Jesus—The Man and His Message

Jesus
The Man
and
His Message

Donald Bridge

Christian Focus Publications

© 1995 Donald Bridge
ISBN 1-85792-117-8

Published by
Christian Focus Publications Ltd
Geanies House, Fearn, Ross-shire,
IV20 1TW, Scotland, Great Britain.

Cover design by Donna Macleod

Printed and bound in Great Britain
by The Guernsey Press Co. Ltd, Vale, Guernsey, C.I.

Contents

Dedication

I dedicate this book to the men of *The Evangelization Society*, better known as TES. The views expressed here are purely my own, but I have the privilege of working with TES in its ministry of bringing the gospel to the people of this nation by every legitimate means, but especially through preaching. To that end, they give their time and energy without reserve. I salute them!

Thanks

I want to express my sincere gratitude to my dear wife Rita. She has added yet more to my immense indebtedness to her, by patiently turning my scribbled longhand into neat typescript. Thank you!

Foreword

Here is a book by Donald Bridge which explores the humanity of our Lord Jesus with diligence and adoration, combining sound theology with pastoral warmth and insight.

It is not enough for us to confess formally that, as God incarnate, Christ is 'wholly God and wholly man'; we must develop fully both sides of that statement if we are to discover and apply the miracle and the message of the gospel. There is no evangelical 'docetism' which is chary of recognising the fullness of our Lord's humanity lest we dishonour him in some way. However there is, finally, no gospel in an incomplete incarnation. Only the Word made flesh can be the Saviour of this world. This is the real Jesus.

Don Bridge has written a book which is often gripping and always challenging, facing us with a Jesus whose company was never easy and whose friendship was never casual:

'In a short public ministry of perhaps three to four years, he outraged every pressure-group, insulted every vested interest and angered every sect and party' (page 105).

In a cry for integrity and truth in a Church where even preachers and leaders can seek popularity and power with a

pared-down gospel he reminds us that Jesus called for disciples not just for decisions—and so must we:

> 'Modern Christian communicators have given way to
> the lure of cheap grace rather than free grace' (page
> 112).

> 'Out of the starkest tragedies of Christian history is the
> Church's failure to embrace the cruciform victory over
> the corrosive influence of power-play' (page 125).

Yet this is also a book which adores Jesus as Lord and God
and touches us with his healing and his hope and a purpose to
know him better and to make him known to our world. Don
Bridge has been doing just that for over forty-three years now
in a ministry which has been in many ways a model for a new
generation of evangelists and pastor-teachers.

Don's full-time ministry began in 1952 at the age of 22
when he joined the *Open Air Mission*, an inter-denomina-
tional, evangelistic organisation. There he learned to 'think
on his feet' preaching at racecourses and outside factory gates
and preaching, incidentally, a thousand times a year in this
period!

After nine years, Don became a lay-pastor at Newcastle-
on-Tyne while studying for the Baptist ministry and in 1965
became pastor of Enon Baptist Church, Sunderland, a church
situated in a tough downtown area and which was, in Don's
words, 'disheartened and non-evangelical'.

Here, Don forged a ministry which was both 'Reformed'
and 'Renewed', combining the strong expository and doctrinal emphasis of an early 'Banner of Truth' man with an

openness to and engagement with 'charismatic' insights and gifts. This experience formed the basis of his most well-known book, co-authored with the Anglican, David Phypers, *Spiritual Gifts and the Church* (IVP 1973 and Christian Focus Publications 1995), a book which sold over 45,000 copies. The church at Sunderland grew to capacity and beyond and another church was planted.

In 1972 Don began a twelve-year ministry at the Frinton Free Church in Essex, a larger and more established evangelical church where Don was to see over 700 people come to Christ. An essential part of that work was the strong emphasis on enquirer's classes or nurture groups which were really a modern equivalent of the old catechising method.

Throughout the years of these ministries Don challenged and encouraged a vision of overseas work as well as home mission and he has been instrumental in the call of well over 200 men and women to home and overseas mission. This global perspective brought him an unusual and high profile ministry in the mid-eighties.

In 1984/5 Don took up a post as chaplain at the Garden Tomb, Jerusalem. Here he preached Sunday by Sunday to congregations of tourists from all over the world numbering from 100-800 and at times reaching 2,000. The period from 1986 to the present has seen Don gather up the wisdom and experience of the past forty-three years in a consultative ministry to church leaders, conferences and local churches large and small, while also teaching at the largest Brethren assembly in Scotland, Riverside Evangelical Church, Ayr (1986-90) and, bringing his ministry full-circle, serving in *The Evangelisation Society* (1990 to the present).

Always astonished that the Lord should use him in such

ways as he has, Don has continually felt the force of Paul's words: 'But we have this treasure in jars of clay to show that the all-surpassing power is from God and not from us'. Indeed he testifies that Paul's second letter to the Corinthians is his 'bible within the Bible' with its emphasis on Paul's weakness and vulnerability. A stern opponent of triumphalism in its various forms, Don Bridge has worked with bodily weakness through most of his adult life, from asthma in youth, through back-pain during most of his ministry to (a good) recovery in recent years from surgery for cancer. An essentially shy man who often dreads the pulpit and the platform, he has to testify to feeling, as well as exhibiting, the anointing of God when he is there.

Don's ministry continues at a pace which would exhaust many younger men and includes, as this book testifies, a writing ministry which has helped thousands through the maze (and sometimes the minefield) of current conflicts and challenges in the Church. His books include *Signs and Wonders Today* (IVP 1985); *Power Evangelism and the Word of God* (Kingsway 1987); *Spare the Rod and Spoil the Church* (Marc Europe 1985) and this book, *Jesus, The Man and his Message*, which I think is one of his best.

I commend it with confidence and with gratitude to God for the long and fruitful ministry of Donald Bridge.

Peter Lewis
The Cornerstone Evangelical Church
Nottingham

Introduction

A word of explanation
This book might well have been called 'Jesus—A Personal View'. Let me explain why, and then give my reasons for settling on a different title.

Since I became a Christian in my early teens, two related ambitions have gripped me. I want to know ever more about that amazing Man who stands at the heart of Christian belief and at the centre of human history. And I long to be ever more skilled and effective in introducing other people to the reality of his living power in their experience.

The pursuit of the first aim has led me to study the Bible for fifty years. Those remarkable books, the Four Gospels, have repeatedly been my centre of gravity. This has involved analysing what they say, exploring where they lead, and applying their lessons to my own lifestyle. That can lead to some surprising conclusions. Did you know that Jesus spoke more about God's judgment than his love? Would you have guessed that he talked about money as often as about God? Have you noticed that he hardly ever mentioned *church* but constantly talked about *Kingdom*? What would you make of the fact that half of the entire story is occupied with the week in which he died? Why did he rarely talk about *conversion* but frequently spoke of *discipleship*? Why did religious leaders dislike him, but bad characters flock to hear him?

The second aim has taken me as a preacher to most cities and towns in England and to several in the rest of Britain. Overseas preaching has led me to Europe, the Middle East, and across the USA. Most movingly it has found me evangelizing and teaching in the places where Jesus walked— Jerusalem, Bethlehem, Nazareth, and the ruins of the Galilee towns of whose destruction he himself warned.

This has brought me back again to my first purpose—to learn all I could of this wondrous figure who stands unique in human history and brings the knowledge of God to all who put their trust in him. Archaeology in Jerusalem, topography around Galilee, history in Judaea, ancient documents found in the desert; all have been grist to my mill, with Bible in hand to check, illumine and confirm.

What has been my overwhelming impression? Simply this, 'These things surely happened. Here is history; here is reality.' Repeatedly one stands at some spot associated with a Jesus-event and reflects, 'I can see why and how it happened here. It is hard to imagine it happening anywhere else.'

Let me not be misunderstood. No-one has to travel to the Middle East to find a sure faith in Christ. Those amazing and incomparable books, the Four Gospels, tell us all we need to know. They not only tell us; they mysteriously (divinely) promote faith. This is why they were written. Luke spells it out. So does John.

'It seemed good to me to write an orderly account .... so that you may know the certainty of the things you have been taught' (Luke 1:1-4).

'These are written that you may believe that Jesus is the

Christ, the Son of God, and that by believing you may have life in his name' (John 20:31).

Certainty—life—these are the promised gifts of Jesus.

This is typical of so many amazing claims made by this carpenter-teacher. Here is a tradesman living in a fairly obscure province of the Roman Empire, a man who never left his own country and culture, who could not lay a finger on the levers of power even there, and who never committed to writing a word of his own. Yet he says to people in every age and culture, dwelling under whatever secular or religious power, 'Trust me. I am worthy of your complete faith and commitment. I can carry anything you put on me. I won't let you down.'

A great deal more than that, too. We hear him claim to be God-made-visible. We see him handing out God's forgiveness. He pulls together all the hopes and aspirations of an ancient people convinced that they had a unique place in God's plan and says 'all this is focused and fulfilled in me'. He calmly announces that he will be the arbiter in the Last Day of Judgment for all mankind. He says the only way to God is through him.

And what he claims, he proves. That, at any rate, is what millions of people living nineteen hundred years later believe and discover.

A well-known British TV star sits in a hotel bedroom, lonely and confused. He picks up one of those ubiquitous Gideon Bibles and reads the words of Jesus. Suddenly he feels able to put his whole trust in that previously far-off figure. Christ became the biggest reality in his life. He says afterwards, '*Now*, I cannot imagine why everyone doesn't believe.'

Two hardened paramilitary terrorists in Northern Ireland,
one 'loyalist' and the other 'republican', sit in separate cells
of the same vast prison, facing up at last to the pointlessness
of their hate-filled lives. Christ becomes real to them, in
pardon and new motives. Having served their sentence, they
join forces to speak and work for peace.

A Jewish atheist in an English university challenges the
Christian Union to a public debate on the physical resurrection of Jesus. Examining the arguments and evidences pro and
con in preparation for the debate, he comes to the astonished
conclusion that *it really happened*—declares himself a Christian and in due course enters the ministry.

The first example is widely known, the second witnessed
by friends of mine, the third is within my personal knowledge.
But none of this depended on a trip to the Holy Land. Of the
millions who today experience and explore that 'life in his
name', only a tiny minority will ever visit Israel, Jordan or
Palestine. They will miss nothing essential to their faith. I
have often teased tourists as I show them some holy site, 'If
you spent £1,000 to come here and find God, I have bad news
and good news for you. The bad news is, you wasted your
money, but the good news is you could have found him at
home—*I* did.'

Then what is the value of walking where Jesus walked? It
underlines the certainty that *the Faith of Christ is based on
fact*. These things really happened. The God who made
mankind and launched it on its seemingly erratic course chose
a time and a place to step in decisively to rescue us from our
predicament. Paul says in Galatians 4:4: 'When the time had
fully come, God sent his Son, born of a woman, born under
law, to redeem (us).' He was 'born of a woman', *that is truly*

human. He was 'born under the law', that is *a member of the Jewish race.* The time, the place and the race were all of God's choosing.

A new member of my congregation in Essex plied me with questions. She was moving away from atheism, and was rather attracted to Eastern religions. She asked me, 'Suppose that Jesus had been born in 800 BC and in India, would Christianity then have been a different shape?' I laughed. 'I can't give you an answer, because that is a non-question. Jesus *couldn't* have been born somewhere else at some other time. He came at the appointed time, to the right place, for a predestined purpose.' And I showed her Paul's words just quoted. Before long she had discovered the truth of it for herself, and in life and death was a radiant witness to the reality of Jesus.

So what is the purpose of this book?
The publishers have asked me to take the readers where Jesus walked and worked, suffered and triumphed, not so much to the places, as to the *circumstances* and the *culture.*

In the last thirty years a flood of information and understanding has become available about the colourful and complex world of Israel in the first century AD. Its examination and interpretation has had some curious results.

Scholars had already engaged for a century in what is often called 'the Quest for the Historical Jesus'. Rejecting the divine inspiration of the Gospel records and expressing a broad dislike of anything supernatural, they have tried to reconstruct a life of Jesus more suited to what they conceived to be modern thought and knowledge. Not surprisingly, they have created imaginary figures in their own image. At the turn of the century Jesus looked suspiciously like a Victorian

Liberal of British or German extraction! Scholars peered down a deep well, glimpsed a distant reflection of themselves, and cried, 'There's Jesus'. How such an anaemic figure could have provoked anyone to crucify him, or inspired anyone to follow him, is equally puzzling.

Since World War 1, 'the New Quest' has majored on speculation as to how the Gospels came to be written. To whom were they addressed? How were the words of Jesus adapted to some supposed situation? Were any of them really the words of Jesus at all? Quite rightly it was emphasised that the Gospels are not biographies but belief-statements. Quite wrongly, that was taken to mean that they were not accurate. It seems an odd idea to me, that because something is written well and with conviction it is unlikely to be true!

The 'Third Quest' began (or at least picked up speed) after World War 2, with the thrilling discovery in the Qumran Caves of Judaea of the Dead Sea Scrolls. The idea arose of taking seriously the history, geography, culture and creeds of the place where Jesus appeared, at the time when he came. Startling parallels with the 'feel' of the New Testament underlined the striking possibility (never abandoned by evangelical Christians) that it might be reliable after all—even 'true'!

One result has been inevitable eccentricities—even blasphemies. Best-selling paperbacks and melodramatic films have offered bizarre reconstructions of 'what Jesus was really like'. They give more striking testimony to their authors' imaginative powers (not to mention their eye on the market) than to any serious handling of facts.

Meanwhile genuine scholars, of all faiths and none, have assembled their discoveries and mustered their arguments.

For twelve months I have paid a fortnightly visit to my local University Bookshop. Every visit has discovered new publications about Jesus—an average of six each visit. Some are by Christians and some by atheists. Some writers are devout traditionalists and some sceptical liberals. A startling number are Jews. Never has the figure of Jesus aroused such intense interest amongst the people to whom he first came, but to whom he has seemed a feared enigma (or worse) for nineteen centuries. Something deeply significant is happening; of that I am sure.

This book is my very modest contribution to 'the Third Quest', unashamedly committed as I am to the inspiration and truth of the Gospel records. I first attempt what might be described as some rough sketches of Jesus. They are personal and selective. I invite you to examine what are *to me* some of the most striking features of this Man who has more followers in today's world than ever before. I keep posing the question 'What is it about him that makes him *good news*?' For that is what *gospel* means. The Christian message does not merely point to a set of propositions about the Son of God who came for our salvation. Nor does it offer redemption through embracing a correct theology of the Atonement and a satisfactory statement of what Jesus did at the cross. It is Christ who saves us—not statements about him.

That leads to a further question—a disturbing one. If Jesus himself *is* the *Evangel* (the Good News) then is he also the ideal *Evangelist* (the communicator of the Good News)? If this Man is himself the heart of the Message, what can we learn of him as Messenger? How does *our* evangelism stand in the light of his message, his methods, his attitudes and his example? I began by saying that I want to know him better *and better to make him known.* So, I assume, does every Christian, not just the professional pastors and evangelists. Well then— as we follow his footsteps do we find the motives, message and methods of the Master reflected in our church life and our personal discipleship? To put it more bluntly—do we ever remind anyone of Jesus?

Chapter 1

The Man who Preached Truth

'God only had one Son, and he made him a preacher,' the Scottish divine Alexander Whyte used to say. The comment is apt. Above all else—above his miracles, his exorcisms, his welcome of the marginalised—Jesus' public preaching was the central factor in that life that led to a cross and an empty tomb—and to our salvation.

It was *the authority of his words* that most amazed people. They observed it in what we still call the *Sermon on the Mount*. His first public act was to announce good news of God's Kingdom and to urge repentance. His parables were breath-catching mini-sermons. His succinct sayings spread like wildfire. His deeds drew people to him, but the words he based on his actions often gave people second thoughts and they turned away again. Puzzled and confused by this, one of his nearest friends commented: 'But to whom would we go if we turn from you? *You have words that give life*' (John 6:68). Temple guards sent to arrest him returned sheepish and empty-handed. 'No-one ever spoke the way this man does,' they declared (John 7:46).

When, much later his arrest was achieved and he stood on trial, it was for *his teaching* (or his alleged teaching) that he was condemned.[1] Quite literally what he taught led him to the cross.

Preaching gets a bad press today. Politicians score emotional points at a party conference, and then explain a few weeks later that (of course) they don't intend to *preach*. For to preach is to pontificate, condemn, cajole and probably to deceive. The presence of twenty American televangelists in prison for fraud during 1991 does little to remove that impression. British churches seem to be losing their confidence in the centrality of the preached word. It is even possible to conduct evangelistic missions (?) without any element of teaching or preaching.

Yet the Christian church has always been at its strongest when following the example of its Master and his apostles who gave prior place to proclamation. In the Gospel records Jesus is described as a *teacher* more than any other title. He is shown preaching on twenty occasions (the apostle Paul eighteen). His message is described as good news. His apostle to the Gentiles insists that God has committed his wisdom and saving power to this unique activity.[2]

> Every preacher, in the measure he preaches the truth as it is in Jesus, and puts on the Lord Jesus Christ, will become clothed with more and more of his Master's authority, and will wield his authority for the same ends.[3]

---

1. Matthew 26:59-66. Luke 23:5, 'He stirs up the people all over Judea by his teaching.' John 18:19, 'The high priest questioned Jesus about his disciples and his teaching.'
2. 'The foolishness of preaching' (1 Corinthians 1:17-25).
3. Alexander Whyte, Lecture 14: 'He taught with authority'.

One message, many voices

We should hasten to add that not all of Christ's preaching was 'sermonising' or 'pulpiteering'. Those activities, powerful though they are, reflect changing cultural trends and mores. What sounds eloquent to one generation seems merely pompous to another. The systematic, lucid exposition of one century can be the boring lecture of the next. After all, even the word 'rhetoric', once a dazzling tribute, is now a near-insult describing the debased content-free pomposities of politicians. The message remains the same, but the style needs to change.

Jesus did sometimes engage in the formal religious preaching of sermons. Luke describes what happened when the newly-famous rabbi returned to the synagogue of his childhood. Every liturgical move is described, as Jesus solemnly stands, receives the proffered scroll, unrolls it, marks the place with a gesture, reads the portion, rolls up the scroll, hands it back to the attendant, and sits in the teacher's seat to give his address. His deliberate omission of the last phrase of the reading creates a stir. His first words of comment are a staggering claim to fulfilment. His eloquence stills the congregation for a time, and then his outrageous application (to them) provokes murderous fury. Here is the pulpit-sermon taking the hearers by the throat or by the hand, as the best of pulpit-preaching has always done. Jesus did this 'throughout Galilee' and had the province by the ears (Matthew 4:23; Luke 4:14-30).

But the natural amphitheatre of sky and hills more often echoed to his words. So did the market place, the crossroads and the quayside. It is hard to imagine that these occasions invited structured sermons. The kind of aphorism, brisk story and colourful parable which we so often see in the Gospel accounts better fits such opportunities than the set piece sermons. The presence of both a 'Sermon on the Mount' in Matthew's account and a 'Sermon on the Plain' in Luke's (Matthew 5-7 and Luke 6) confirms the fact that he gave similar basic talks with varying contents as the occasion required. Mark records with obvious delight the frequent times when an incident or a challenge is turned by Jesus into a dazzling succinct saying, like 'I came not to call the righteous but sinners' or 'the Son of Man came not to be served but to serve' (Mark 2:17; 10:45).

This *ad hoc* grasping of an incident to underline a truth, is of the very essence of open-air preaching. In the days when I preached outdoors more than in (about one thousand times each year), I deliberately studied and tried to emulate Jesus' technique. It calls for a sense of humour, a ready rapport with people, a keen eye for simile, and a quick grasp of the essential situation. Plus, of course, the ability to make biblical truth relevant.

A fascinating example of outdoor incident leading to pronouncement, then to debate, and then to formal preaching in the synagogue, is found in John's account of the feeding of the five thousand. It is filled with human interaction, and also provides some of those unintended coincidences that so clearly mark a truthful record (John 6:1-59).

The Passover Feast is near. The miracle is performed. The crowd become agitated. Revolutionary elements see this as a chance to 'make him king by force'. (Another coincidence here: Matthew tells us without explanation that Jesus first pressed the disciples to leave in the boat, then dismissed the crowd single-handed, and went alone into the mountain to pray. The disciples could not be trusted with the temptation of political populism, and Jesus himself needed to pray against that temptation to seize lordship without suffering, which pursued his steps from the beginning to the end. But John, who omits the detail, actually gives the reason: the excitement of the political Zealots—John 6:15, cf. Matthew 14:22-23.)

Then follows the incident of the storm on the lake, which reunites Jesus and the disciples. Next morning, back on the quayside at Capernaum, he takes up the theme of miraculous bread again, and applies its lessons. A 'pronouncement' ('eternal life the Son of Man will give you') leads to a prolonged discussion with questions and answers—all of it totally typical of the kind of three-sided rabbi-disciples-onlookers dialogue which we now know was common at that time.

Then at some point the scene changes, to our surprise. 'He said this while teaching in the synagogue in Capernaum' (John 6:59). Apparently it is now the Sabbath. The discussion has pursued its course whilst the rabbi walks from harbour to synagogue (about a quarter-mile: the remains of both can still be seen) surrounded by the excited crowd. Now, from the preacher's seat, the teaching-sermon continues, in a rather more formal style, readily recognisable from the Dead Sea Scrolls and from rabbinical literature. Like every good communicator, Jesus adapts style and vocabulary to occasion and audience.

Moreover, his Old Testament references and allusions are the very scriptures which we know from the Mishnah to be the chosen portions read in the run-up to Passover: another adaptation of style to circumstance. And now we see the force of another unintended coincidence, for verse 10 says 'there was plenty of green grass in that place'. But the only time when that obtains is the run-up to Passover, after the cold winter rains but before the burning sun of summer. And verse 4 tells us 'the Jewish Passover was near'!

The greatest rabbi

What all of this shows us is a fairly typical rabbi-pattern of preaching, teaching, dialogue and argument—but with a hugely significant difference. Itinerant rabbis were a popular feature in first century Judaea, though less so in Galilee. The word simply means *teacher*, and at this point in time was not used as an honorific title.

We shall be looking at the rabbis again. Sufficient for the moment to establish that most of them in Jesus' time were of the Pharisee party, although in Galilee there would be a conservative suspicion of the newfangled 'traditions' added to scripture by their more sophisticated southern brethren. We may imagine a rabbi walking into the village accompanied by his mobile 'school' of disciples. Visitors are news-carriers and therefore always welcome. A crowd gathers. The teacher displays his sheepskin diploma with its authority from his more senior and famous mentor. He might exercise a simple healing ministry (a mixture of naturopathy, prayer and exorcism). He may get straight to the point, with chanted scriptures and pithy comments, often anecdotal and meta-phorical.

But there the likeness ends. People were astonished at Jesus' visits because he was not like 'the other teachers of the law' (Matthew 7:28-29). The difference lay in his authority—and their lack of it. A rabbi's task was to quote those who had gone before him, to comment on the quotations, to balance one argument with another, to match one precedent against another, to muster all the convoluted attempts to strengthen (or to weaken) God's commands as revealed in the Law (the Torah). The result was an endless debate, a maze of alternative pathways (somewhat ironically described as Halakah—the way).

It is possible to exaggerate the weaknesses of this approach, and Protestant Christians have sometimes done that. When Dean Farrar wrote in 1906 of their 'meddling, carnal, superficial spirit of word-weaving and letter-worship, spinning large accumulations of worthless subtlety all over the Mosaic code which turned ten commands into six hundred and thirteen' he was describing the worst rather than the average, and expressing the distaste of a Liberal English Protestant to boot.[4] Nevertheless, Jesus accused them of emptying God's Word of its power with their human traditions, and during his last week in Jerusalem castigated some of them as hypocrites and worse.[5]

The point is—his contemporaries spoke with confusion, indecision and divided opinion: he spoke with crisp authority. They quoted 'it is written' and 'it is suggested'. He announced 'I say unto you'. He even changed the use of the word *Amen*! Hitherto it always followed a prayer, and meant rather wistfully 'may it be so—I hope so'. He (and no-one else) prefaced his sentences with it, and made it mean 'This is so, for I am

---

4. Farrar, Chapter 18, *The Twelve and the Sermon on the Mount.*
5. Matthew 15:1-9; Matthew 23 (entire chapter). The word hypocrite (literally 'play-actor') did not imply deliberate conscious deceit, but rather an overemphasis on external appearance and outward observance.

telling you'. Hence the rather appealing, if archaic, Authorised Version, 'Verily, verily I say unto you'. Today's equivalent would be 'This is the truth—you can be sure' (John
5:19;10:1, Authorised Version).

Authority, then. This was the mark of Christ's preaching.
He spoke because he knew. He knew because the Father, with
whom he lived in perfect harmony, had told him so. Like the
carpenter Joseph who taught his boy the craft behind locked
doors, 'the Father loves the Son and shows him all he does. The
Son can do nothing by himself: he can only do what he sees
his Father doing' (John 5:19-20). When Jesus entered a
village (as Mark and Luke constantly demonstrate) it must
have looked at first like the advent of yet another rabbi, an
object of interest, speculation or debate to one or another of
the inhabitants. But all soon came to sense that, if he was to
be taken seriously at all, one stood before them who brought
the very truth of God—not for discussion and debate, but to
stimulate penitence, faith and adoring obedience.

This was Jesus the preacher: the man with authority. The
church and its leaders express and reflect that authority when,
and only when, they are faithful to his Word, in message and
in manner of life.

This authority in preaching is not a matter of position in a
religious hierarchy. An archbishop does not have more of it
than an archdeacon. An Assembly Moderator does not display
more of it than a Presbyterian minister. It is not given to
Baptist pastors, but withheld from deacons!

Nor is it granted automatically by formal theological
training, which all too often resembles the 'on one hand, on
the other hand' of the rabbinical schools, with authority as the
first casualty.

Nor does it depend on communication skills, important though they are. A polished presentation with overhead projector or background music may help to communicate, but it adds nothing to divine authority. The manipulative skills of certain televangelists and would-be mass-pulpiteers may have much to do with persuasion, but they have little to do with authority.

Authority in preaching springs from *total confidence in the written Word of God*. It is displayed in a handling of that Word which reflects the character, glory and servanthood of Jesus. It is exercised by those to whom God sovereignly chooses to give it; people who spend much time in prayer for wisdom in preparation and unction in delivery. Mere orthodoxy, essential though that is, will never be sufficient for the preacher who longs for spiritual power. He burns to see the Word applied in practical, measurable effectiveness. Do the hearers change their attitudes? Do they come to faith? Do they flee from lust and pride, and seek after holiness?

Tragically, many evangelicals have lost confidence in authoritative, biblical preaching. It is denigrated, even gently rubbished. Some Christians, it would seem, would rather see wonders than hear truth. Some get excited by a two-minute word of knowledge that reveals a blue-eyed man with an ingrowing toenail, but are bored by a Spirit-anointed, thirty-minute exposition of John chapter 5 that reveals the wonder of God's Son. Some ministers rate skilled administration higher than powerful preaching, preferring a morning seated at the computer among the files to a morning on their knees with an open Bible.

Now of course, healing, words of knowledge and spiritual administration are all valued charismata. Some Christians are called to exercise those gifts and talents, just as others are called to preach and teach. Nevertheless, when it comes to *priority* there can be no comparison. The church is called to follow its Master in the proclamation of good news. To abandon that exercise is to abandon an essential factor in the earthly and heavenly ministry of the Son of God.

'God had only one Son, and he made him a preacher.'

Chapter 2

The Man who Mastered Words

When we picture Jesus preaching and teaching, we have to put as far behind us as we can, the Hollywood epic and TV image. No blond-haired orator who speaks either Kennedy-American or BBC-English. No background of orchestral music and occasional angelic choirs. Jesus was the master-communicator. He handled words with the brilliant skill of one who is rightly called THE WORD of GOD—the Creator's self-revelation in voice and lifestyle (John 1:1-14, cf. Hebrews 1:1-3).

The modern idea that *the medium is the message* is a typically cynical product of an age that knows no absolute truths because man, not God, is made the measure of all things. So slogans, newspaper headlines, soundbites, TV jingles, 'commercials' and subliminal suggestive advertising replace truth and fact. We, the victims, can become almost incapable of serious thought or moral decision.

Jesus communicated—but not like that. His media skills depended on the truth that he conveyed, the integrity with which he spoke, and the lifestyle which backed his words. Nevertheless, he did make brilliant use of word, phrase, sentence and simile. He had several techniques. Truth does not have to be boring, and it never was when he spoke it.

Jesus' language was, we can be almost sure, a variety of Western Semitic, called *Aramaic*; pure Hebrew was reserved for the reading of Scripture, in which it was written, and perhaps for the chanting of liturgical prayers. The dialect of Galilee was related to classical Hebrew very much as broad Yorkshire or Geordie to Shakespeare's English. This is not a facetious suggestion: Galilee was precisely the industrial northeast of Palestine, the industries being intensive farming in the warm black volcanic soil, and intensive fishing whose dried products were sold in far-off Rome under the European and Middle Eastern common market imposed by the Caesars. Twenty-six actual Aramaic words of Jesus are embedded in the Greek text of the Gospel records. The more famous are given verbatim, because of their dramatic implications.[1]

Down in the sophisticated southern cities, and especially in Jerusalem, a more gentlemanly Aramaic was spoken, intermixed with purer Hebrew (rather as Home Counties MPs or Oxford and Cambridge dons will sprinkle their speech with apt quotations from Latin or Greek). In contrast, the dialect of Jesus' Galilee was broad, heavily accented, and the butt of a good deal of condescending humour. Gutterals were a problem to Galileans. To put it bluntly, they had trouble with their 'aitches'. Peter was instantly spotted when he tried to slip into the high priest's courtyard after Jesus' arrest— because of his dialect.[2] Two hundred years later Babylonian

---

1. Joachim Jeremias pages 9-12. However, some scholarly opinion (including Jewish) is swinging back to the opinion that Jesus spoke fluent 'classical Hebrew' which can be distinguished in the Gospels more often than the Aramaic. See David Jackman, page 13.
2. Peter's dialect. Matthew 26:69-75. See verse 73 'your accent gives you away.'

rabbis scornfully suggested that Galileans lapsed into false doctrine because they couldn't pronounce God's Word properly.

Jesus' own pronunciation of *Lazarus* (in the healing of his friend and the parable of Hades) was actually a 'mispronunciation' by southern standards—the 'correct' word is *Eleazar*. One of the traditional jibes about 'stupid Galileans' (as they were often dubbed) was that you could never tell whether they were asking for a donkey, a drink, a jacket or a lamb (hamaar, hamar, amar or immar). Even when the dying Jesus called on God in Galilean Aramaic [Eloi, Eloi] the onlookers either pretended to misunderstand or genuinely misunderstood, and said he was crying to Elias [Elijah] (Matthew 27:45-50).

Yet, like Geordie or Yorkshire, the Galilean dialect had communication advantages. It was singsong, colourful, humorous, and rich with idiom. It fell naturally into rhyme and, in a mainly non-reading culture, that offered great help in memorising. Jesus' teaching is full of this rhyming, rhythmical, poetic, repetitive style.

> Ask and it will be given to you;
> Seek and you will find;
> Knock and the door will be opened to you;
> For everyone who asks receives;
> He who seeks finds;
> And to him who knocks, the door will be opened
> (Matthew 7:7-8).
>
> The rain came down
> the streams rose
> the winds blew
> Yet (this) house did not fall.

The rain came down
the streams rose
the winds blew
And (that house) fell with a crash (Matthew 7:24-27).

Christ's words have been analysed and classified with
meticulous care by scholars who know enough of the language
to do so. They come up with statistics like 'one hundred and
eight antithetic parallelisms' and so on. Lower mortals can
recognise the power and colour without being able to define
the technicalities. Jesus, simply, was a genius with words.
Memorable, colourful, onomatopoeic, musical, vivid, terse—
above all, Christ's words were charged with power.

Craftsman with words

'He's not like a proper bishop: you can understand what he
says.' The complaint was made of John Charles Ryle, first
Bishop of Liverpool. It reflected an idea quite widely held in
religious circles, that to be obscure is a sign of profundity.
Professor F F Bruce of Manchester recalled conference
speakers heard in his Brethren youth: 'Some hearers had the
idea that a speaker was not much good if they could understand all he said. They felt they were getting their money's
worth if he was some way above their heads.'

Not so with Jesus. His purpose was to communicate, not to
confuse. He used every legitimate verbal device to illuminate
his message. If people rejected his words, it was not because
they misunderstood him, but because they understood him
only too well. He employed an astonishing variety of verbal
tactics to catch the attention, grip the conscience and capture
the imagination of his hearers.

Jesus was master of *the pithy one-liner*. 'Blessed are the pure in heart, for they will see God.' Safe assertion, since only the pure in heart will have any desire to! Recall *the pungent phrases* like 'Many are called but few are chosen'. Think of *the wry comments* like 'Each day has enough trouble of its own'. Puzzle over the *outrageous warning* against throwing pearls to pigs. Wince at *the unforgettable epigram* that the first shall be last, and the last come first. Here are words that stick because of brevity and paradox (Matthew 5:8; 22:14; 6:34; 7:6; 20:16).

His deliberate exaggerations must have drawn appreciative chuckles, followed by thoughtful frowns as their import sank in. Teasing overstatement (*hyperbole*) has always been stock-in-trade for storytellers. Indeed, Jesus' picture of someone fussing to extract a speck of sawdust from a friend's eye whilst a great plank sticks unnoticed in his own, had several near-equivalents amongst the more liberal rabbis of his day.[3]

Cultural Reflections

Like any other good commentator (but incomparably better) Jesus constantly referred to current customs and contemporary events. Read any good background book to biblical Israel, and every page will remind you a dozen times of the words of Christ. He drew his illustrations from Joseph's carpentry shop, Mary's kitchen, Zebedee's fishing-business, Levi's tax office, Martha's portable flour-mill. He pointed up pungent truths from cornfield and marketplace, from city street and flower-flung field.

---

3. Jesus' hyperbole compared with contemporary rabbis: cf. Hilton & Marshall, *The Gospels and Rabbinic Judaism*. At a simpler level: Walter Riggans, *Jesus ben Joseph*.

In the News

Topical events were grist to his mill, and items 'in the news' were quoted as illustrations of profound truths. A modern evangelist will often sprinkle his preaching with allusions to politicians, filmstars, novelists or television advertisers— not of course as authorities, but by way of familiar warning and example. In similar fashion, Jesus seems to have alluded to the errors, antics and exploits of people famous or familiar in first century Palestine. His hearers must have tittered—and sometimes glanced uneasily over their shoulders as they did so.

'Suppose one of you wants to build a tower' (he begins a lesson on the need for thought-out commitment) and follows with a thinly-veiled reference to Governor Pilate's blunder in thinking he could plunder temple funds to build an aqueduct. He then repeats the point with a scarcely-disguised reference to King Herod having to call off a war with a neighbour because his army was too small (Luke 14:28-33).

Pilate's bloody repression of a rebellion, the collapse of a building in Jerusalem, and the tragic news of a prophet's murder were other events from current news bulletins on which he drew (Luke 13:1-5).

The Power of Word-pictures

Aristotle taught that the command of metaphor is the greatest thing by far in effective communication. Macneil Dixon goes so far as to call it the most powerful force in the making of history. In fact the 'likening' of an unfamiliar thing to a familiar is fundamental to the very use of words and the sharing of ideas. 'Well, it's like this,' we say. How else can we proceed to the unknown than from the known?

Jesus was master of the 'like this'. The Kingdom of God

is *like* ... a farmer whose sneaky enemy tries to ruin his crop; *like* ... a tiny seed sown to produce a huge plant; *like* ... a touch of yeast that makes the whole baking rise. All of these metaphors, plus that of a treasure hunt, a jewel collector and a fisherman with a very mixed catch, appear in one short section of Matthew's account (chapter 13).

Transference (which is the literal meaning of the idea of metaphor) is of the very essence of Christ's teaching. And it was, significantly, the life of ordinary people (Mr and Mrs Average) which supplied him with his material. Hardly any of his analogies are religious: most are secular. Few are drawn from urban life and most are rural. The harvest field, village wedding, market square, kitchen, bakery, lakeside, meadow path: these are the scenes from which he draws the profoundest truths about God and his Kingdom. There is a divine pattern in the created world and especially the world of people. The Creator and Redeemer are one. Human life reflects divine principles: our cares and concerns mirror the mind of God (though of course the mirror is clouded and the image warped by sin). Ordinary life furnishes pointers to God's rule, which Jesus calls the Kingdom of God.

He urged his followers to behave like sparrows, slaves, household managers, bridesmaids, children and students (e.g. Matthew 6:26; 10:24). In one glorious collection of truly mixed metaphors, he urged them to resemble sheep, snakes and doves all at once (Matthew 10:16). In the Sermon on the Mount alone, he compared those who take his message seriously to: beggars, mourners, salt, table-lamps, plaintiffs in court, householders threatened by burglars, birds, flowers, carpenters, travellers, sheep, fruit trees and building contractors (Matthew 5-7).

He described himself in a cascade of similes from the religious world, the political world, and the household scene. For example, from Luke's account we can extract almost at random, self-portraits of Jesus as Son of God, doctor, Elijah, Elisha, son of man, bridegroom, wine-seller, rich man throwing a party, shepherd, housewife, loving father, and estate manager. Several of these similes (doctor, bridegroom, shepherd) were already in religious use as metaphors for God; an observation which did not escape his hearers' attention.

The common tongue: many of Jesus' words were coined in the idiom of Hebrew or Aramaic, and can only make sense in that context. Idiom is in turn closely related to slang. That may irritate linguistic purists (and cause problems to well-meaning builders of religious liturgy), but the fact is that idiom and slang enrich and enliven speech with the language of the here-and-now, the verbal-coinage of pavement and market place. Both idiom and slang can be illuminating, humorous and relevant—to those familiar with it. Hearers from another culture find it somewhat confusing. What do you mean by 'cheer up', 'don't be two-faced' or 'let your hair down'? The list is endless, and it can be quite difficult to find alternative non-idiomatic phrases (as anyone who has preached through an interpreter discovers). Jesus' teaching is crowded with such idiomatic colour.

His warning about an 'evil eye' refers to a mean disposition. The reference to pearls before pigs is another piece of idiom, as is the startling suggestion that there are appropriate reasons for cutting off your hand and tearing out your eye. Strange words about hating those nearest to you find meaning in the Hebrew concept of 'loving less'. 'An eye for an eye' is another example of idiom with a Bible background and Jesus' riposte to that was another piece of idiom, 'turn the other cheek', which is still a part of modern English slang. Every Gospel reader will be able to think of others—moving mountains, giving snakes to children, pushing a camel through a needle's eye, giving bread to dogs, etc., etc.[4]

The Humour of Jesus

The Teacher from Nazareth could be very funny. That may not be immediately obvious to a modern western reader. Indeed, the very suggestion of humour in Jesus may shock some Christians, and for several reasons.

First, the nature of fun changes with time. Try reading those ancient copies of *Punch* in the dentist's waiting room!

Secondly, cultural factors greatly influence our concept of humour. I once extricated myself from a nasty situation with an Arab in Old Jerusalem simply by bursting into spontaneous mirth. What provoked anger in him, struck me as hilarious—and this was so confusing that he and his threatening friends backed off in bewilderment.

Thirdly, Christians can have problems with the humanity of Jesus. They struggle with a genuinely human figure who could feel hunger, thirst, tiredness, anger, grief—and amusement.

Fourthly, much humour has become perverted, cruel, unjust and sinful. It shares our fallen-ness. Jesus was perfect man and therefore his humour was perfect and unsullied. But that is hard for us to imagine even as a possibility.

Fifthly, the solemn, awesome elements in the Jesus-story can make us hesitate. Most of us have heard the unfortunate comment, 'We read that Jesus wept, but never that he laughed'. Isaiah's prophetic description of 'a man of sorrows, ac-

---

4. Scattered throughout Luke 3, 5, 14-16.

quainted with grief' can become a kind of overall image of a
Saviour who never smiled. But this is a half-truth, a well-
meaning but misleading caricature. Read the story with
sympathetic imagination, and smiles are obvious. Consider
the word-picture of the man who fussily extracts a speck of
dust from his workmate's eye whilst ignoring a plank sticking
in his own. Smile wryly at the dinner guest who loudly
complains of a gnat in his soup, but absent-mindedly swal-
lows a camel. Here are gentle jokes with a serious point.[5]

The basis of humour is, I suggest, *the perception of the
ridiculous*. This, in turn, springs from a sense of proportion.
Something is hilariously absurd if it is badly out of proportion. Irony and satire underline the fact that something is
contradictory and out of kilter.

Jesus, the perfect man, was the most balanced and well
proportioned. Therefore his sense of humour was perfect.

Modern readers puzzle over the parable of the sacked
servant who slid out of the worst consequences of his misdeed
(Luke 16:1-9). What exactly is it that Jesus can possibly
commend in the wily rogue? The original hearers, who would
have been almost entirely on the rascal's side, would greet the
story with slapped thighs and appreciative chuckles—as in
effect does the estate manager himself in the parable. No
doubt Matthew, the converted tax-collector, laughed loudest.

The danger of taking yourself far too seriously is the target
for much of Christ's teasing. The absurd philanthropist who
blows a trumpet before slipping a gift to charity; the religious
man who scuffs his clothes, dirties his face and rumples his

---

5. Jesus' humour: Matthew 7:1-6; 23:24. Cf. *Humour and Irony in the
New Testament* by Jakob Jonsson.

hair in order to tell everyone that he is secretly fasting and praying; those ridiculous people ignoring planks and swallowing camels; all suffer the same lack of perspective about themselves. Their unimpressive virtues are obvious to them; their alarming vices they ignore. Nor is this merely a minor point. *For to receive God's grace we must abandon false confidence in ourselves.*

Which is exactly what Jesus meant by his smiling question: 'Who fills a doctor's waiting room? Fit people, or those who know they are sick?'

Proportion—perspective—incongruence—paradox: all of these are ingredients of humour, as is the joy of being able to see life in its right proportions, however dark some of the colours may be. Jewish humour (*chotzner*) still abounds with this self-deprecating element, which goes all the way back to the satire of the proverbs and the prophets—and finds modern expression in people as diverse as Rabbi Lionel Blue and comedian-director Woody Allen.

It is no coincidence that John in his great prologue calls Jesus Christ, THE WORD.

In the beginning was the Word
and the Word was with God
and the Word was God...

The Word became flesh and made
his dwelling among us.
We have seen his glory (John 1:1, 14).

The word *logos* (Word) would strike vibrating chords in different readers, depending on their culture and background.

To mainline Jews, God's creative *word* of command brought the universe into being. His moral *commands* enlighten the confused and sinful heart. His *voice* through the prophets gives understanding and application in everyday life and in the great crises of the nation. To a rather mystical and speculative Jewish movement in contemporary Egypt, the Logos of God was believed to have such power that it could be described in personal terms. To Greeks, who were inclined to believe in the likelihood of one supreme god, but who knew little about him, the idea prevailed of his logos (mind = word = self-expression) somehow making itself known.[6]

During my residence in Jerusalem I often discussed theology with a bishop of the ancient 'Church of the East', a breakaway from the Melkite Church which traces its roots right back to the earliest Galilean Christians, celebrates Passover, and keeps its scriptures and liturgical prayers in the original language of Jesus. (The bishop was a Scotsman, though how that came to be I cannot imagine, and never liked to ask!) He once explained to me how effectively he could dialogue with both Jews and Muslims about the person of Jesus, if he employs the biblical metaphor of Logos-Word rather than the equally biblical metaphor of Father-Son. To a Jew, claims for a 'Son of God' sound like instant threats to his passionate belief in One God. To a Muslim it sounds even worse, for he has been taught that Father-Son must imply sexual activity in God. But Jewish rabbinical writings (with roots in the very time of Jesus) speak in startlingly personal ways of God's *Word*, God's *Wisdom* and God's *Law* as if describing an individual. And to a lesser degree, Muslim

---

6. James Dunn, *The Partings of the Ways*, chapter 11.

tradition speaks of God's verbal activity in somewhat personal terms.[7]

When Jesus spoke, people heard the voice of God. No wonder they marvelled at his verbal authority and said 'no-one else ever spoke like this man'. At the end of the twentieth century we are surrounded by a hundred conflicting voices. They unite only to affirm that there is no such thing as Truth. We are offered a pick-'n-mix from which we may choose what appeals to us. We are told that the only truth is 'what is true for me'. Total subjectivism holds sway. Choose your own sexual morality. Choose your own lifestyle. Does it feel good? Then do it and believe it.

Communicating the Truth today

What can the modern Christian learn from Christ's deployment of anecdote and analogy, his skill with words, his humour and his parables? Surely this, at least. It is not enough to *proclaim*: we must *communicate*.

We have seen how highly Jesus rated preaching, yet how many other ways he communicated in addition to the way of the set-piece sermon. His purpose was to grip the attention, engage the conscience and inform the mind. Mere faithfulness to the 'sound' of truth (the time-honoured phrases) was not enough. It could be said of him as was said of one of his greatest apostles:

> Our gospel came to you not simply with words, but also with power, with the Holy Spirit, and with deep conviction (1 Thessalonians 1:5).

---

7. Bridge, *Living In The Promised Land*, pages 115-145.

To achieve that purpose, Jesus did not reason 'truth has its own inbuilt power; I need only declare it, with no attempt to illustrate, explain, simplify and apply'. Rather he used the dialect of the common people, drew illustrations from their ordinary lives, referred often to current events, deployed humour, and laboured to make his truth pungently relevant.

Deeply though he believed in the divine inspiration of the Old Testament (which is why we do, too) he rarely gave extended quotations from it in accepted 'religious language'. He used his Bible allusively ('As it was in the days of Noah', 'As Moses lifted up the serpent in the desert', 'As the Queen of Sheba travelled to meet Solomon', 'As the commandment says, Do not kill' - etc.). Or he used it indirectly (simply referring in 'modern' stories to doctors, vineyards, shepherds, bridesmaids etc., knowing that all of these words echoed Old Testament truths about God and his people).

I know an evangelist who communicates brilliantly in today's society, especially in 'the media' (secular magazines, popular TV chat-shows or current-affairs programmes). Many people 'out there' discern God's truth and Christ's compassion in what this man says and does. His most bitter critics are earnest evangelical Christians. They write to editors or directors to complain, 'He never mentioned the blood of Christ', 'He doesn't spell out the Atonement', 'He hardly ever quotes the Bible'. Such critics are failing to recognise the distinction between *stating* the truth and *communicating* it. They apparently expect to hear the whole counsel of God (or perhaps the Apostles' Creed) enunciated in a three-minute 'spot' devoted to Bosnia, AIDS or the plight of the homeless. But the same criticism could be levelled at two-thirds of the recorded words of Jesus.

One of the finest talks on the uniqueness of Jesus I have ever heard was given by a preacher renowned for his 'Reformed doctrine' and his suspicions of modern music. Yet he prepared it by scribbling a few words on the paper table-napkin during a dinner in a yacht-club bar and restaurant. He delivered it to an intensely interested audience, the air thick with smoke and heavy with alcoholic fumes. He went his way, and I spent a week pursuing further the striking contacts made. He rarely *quoted scripture*, but his talk, couched in today's terms, was totally *biblical*.

I have often had to attempt the same. On a racecourse one can profitably(!) use the name of a runner. In the market-square a newspaper headline may be the starting point. In a youth club, some knowledge of the local favourite football team will be useful. Back in that same yacht-club I spoke about sailing, then about Galilee (on which I've sailed) and then about Jesus. At a Rotary club beside Lake Ozark in Missouri, I compared Ozark Town with Capernaum (there are several likenesses) and went on to explain God's way of salvation. In all of these places, people have found the living Christ. There was communication. We need to follow the Master in this, as in every other example.

Nor is this task committed only to professional preachers. Peter's great words gripped me before I ever dreamt of pulpits (or racecourses) and led me into natural witnessing:

In your hearts set apart Christ as Lord. Always be prepared to give an answer to everyone who asks you to give the reason for the hope that you have. But do this with gentleness and respect (1 Peter 3:15-16).

Chapter 3

The Man who Broke Barriers

The thing that shocked people about Jesus was his choice of friends. To put it mildly, he was not very particular about the company he kept. In that single fact lies the heart of his gospel.

Within a few paragraphs of the start, Mark's account shows the Master in trouble for this very reason:

> Many tax collectors and 'sinners' were eating with him and his disciples .... When the teachers of the law who were Pharisees saw him eating with the 'sinners' and tax-collectors, they asked his disciples: 'Why does he eat with (them)?'

Jesus responded with one of those typical sayings that stick to the memory like a burr to a coat sleeve.

> It is not the healthy who need a doctor, but the sick. I have not come to call the righteous, but 'sinners' (Mark 2:13-17).

It was always happening. His closest school of disciples included a renegade tax-collector (Matthew) and an ex-supporter of urban guerilla terrorists (Simon). His wider circle contained several women, at a time when pious Jews thanked God that they were neither lepers, Gentiles nor women. On one embarrassing occasion a woman with a loose moral reputation burst into a party, anointed Christ's feet with scent, bathed them in her tears, and wiped them with her unbound hair (itself an accepted sign of immodesty). Not at all the right kind of people![1]

'This man welcomes sinners and eats with them' was the scornful accusation of his religious enemies (Luke 15:1-2). Eating together was a deeply significant act of piety, friendship and acceptance. You judged a man by what he ate, how he ate it, and who he ate it with. Jesus blatantly ignored this accepted wisdom. He discouraged excessive concern about food 'purity' laws, cheerfully accepted invitations to meals with very dubious characters, encouraged a kind of conversion-celebration-meal when he called new disciples from doubtful backgrounds, and introduced a sacramental meal as an act of worship and remembrance on the very eve of his death.

The early church had a hard time coming to terms with this, as the Acts of the Apostles and several New Testament letters eloquently indicate (Acts 15:19-21; Romans 14; Galatians 2:11-14).

But who exactly were these 'sinners' with whom Christ so scandalously ate? Modern evangelicals, aware of the apostolic teaching that 'all have sinned' and none is naturally good, have slightly misunderstood the implications.

---

1. Luke 7:36-50. The incident led to one of Christ's greatest 'grace' parables—that of The Two Debtors.

> Sinners Jesus will receive
>> Sound this word of grace to all
> Who the heavenly pathway leave
>> All who falter, all who fall

so sang our Sankey-taught grandparents. In other words, God has a just quarrel with all who offend his holy law, but in amazing grace has opened a way of return to himself through the gift of his Son. This is true, and needs to be said. But it is not what Jesus was saying when he gained the scandalous reputation of 'The Son of Man, eating and drinking ... a glutton and a drunkard, and a friend of tax collectors and "sinners" ' (Luke 7:34; 15:1-7).

Jesus himself never referred to people as sinners, except when quoting his critics (and half-derisively describing them in turn as 'the righteous'). Closer to the word as the critics employed it ('sinners' in quotation marks, as the New International Version helpfully renders it) is the attitude echoed in rather earlier hymns. The Wesley brothers in the eighteenth century sang:

> Come sinners to the gospel feast,
>> Let every soul be Jesus' guest;
> Ye need not one be left behind
>> For God hath bidden all mankind.

(A marvellous hymn which goes on to paraphrase the whole 'feast parable' of Luke 14, including all the lame excuses given for refusing the invitation.) Even more specifically the great hymn 'Where shall my wondering soul begin?' accurately identifies the 'sinners':

Outcasts of men, to you I call
   Harlots and publicans and thieves!
He spreads his arms to embrace you all;
   Sinners alone his grace receive;
No need of him the righteous have;
   He came the lost to seek and save.

Outcasts—that reflects exactly what the word 'sinners' implied when on the lips of Christ's scandalised opponents.

Evangelists like the Wesleys were acutely aware that their preaching and practice, like that of their Saviour, attracted the poor, the despised, the criminals and the marginalised. Men sprawled in drinking-houses ('drunk for a penny, dead drunk tuppence, straw free'), criminals facing execution in reeking prisons, women forced into prostitution to feed their families, children living in coalmines ... these were the people who began to press into parish-church communion services to the embarrassment and distaste of the respectable.

The marginalised: that phrase best sums up what Christ's critics meant by 'sinners'. To the Jewish establishment (with good biblical precedent) sin implied not only personal misdemeanour but also *separation from God's holy people*, exclusion from the godly community. By definition, *Gentiles* were outside. So were *Samaritans*, those embarrassing half-breeds. *Galileans* (only a century old in their Jewish commitment and inclined to ride loosely to Jerusalem tradition) were half in and half out. Then of course all *women* were in an equivocal position (with a separate court provided in the temple, and a separating curtain in the synagogues). And what of those who compromised Jewish purity either *politically* (like tax collectors) or *morally* (like the persistently promiscuous) or *inadvertently* (through physical contamination)?

The great symbols of Jewish identity, highly valued because they were so overt and easily definable, were Sabbath Observance and the Laws of Purity, especially those associated with food and eating-utensils. Only 150 years in the past towered the stirring, emotive example of the Maccabean period. Then, warriors, priests and martyrs had made those symbols the supreme test of loyalty when the very identity of God's chosen people was under threat from Greek religion and military might. How you spend the seventh day, what you eat, how you eat it, and in whose company you eat it; how you avoid ceremonial defilement—these were issues of life and death—sometimes literally. Play fast and loose with these, and you insulted the memory of the martyrs. Ignore or defy these, and you cast a giant question mark over your right to be regarded as members of God's Israel.

'Sinners', then, were those whose ignorance, carelessness or deliberate non-observance threatened the identity of God's People. Then, by extension and gradually, the word came to mean 'those who are outside of my group or party'. Pharisees dismissed the less strict populace as 'the cursed mob who know nothing of the law' (John 7:49). Essenes very much doubted whether the Pharisees themselves scraped inside!

Exclusion could be on grounds of *health* (leprosy, internal bleeding and demon possession), on grounds of *race* (Gentiles) and on grounds of *religion* (Samaritans). *Gender* was a problem: women were often excluded simply because they were feminine. Certain forms of *employment* raised barriers: tax-collectors who benefited the godless authorities; tanners who unavoidably touched blood. It is no accident that Peter was lodging with a tanner when Providence drove him further 'out' to a Roman household.[2] *Morality*, of course, was a boundary line not easily crossed ('a woman who was a sinner' almost certainly means a prostitute). Finally, *party* defined the barriers (as with Pharisees, Essenes and Zealots).

This is the context in which Jesus extended his astonishing, infuriating invitation 'Come to me—walk with me—eat with me'. In one breathless series of events described (typically) by Mark, he offered forgiveness to a paralysed man, called a tax-collector to follow him, presided at a celebration-party attended by the most notorious characters, dismissed the Pharisees' extra rules about fasting, warned of new wine that burst out of old skins, encouraged a very relaxed attitude to Sabbath regulations, healed a man on the Sabbath, and appointed an inner circle of 'apostles', at least two of whom were rank outsiders (Mark 2, 3). By that time his critics couldn't decide whether he was mad, possessed, or simply a target for assassination!

Says Professor James Dunn of Durham, 'He came to call precisely those whom the most religious of his fellow-Jews rejected as having put themselves outside the scope of God's covenant provision'.[3] Jesus not only dismissed the accusa-

---

2. Acts 9:43; 10:9-18, 27-29, 44-48. Borg lists seven occupations that automatically disqualified people as unclean or 'most-despised': gamblers with dice, usurers, organisers of games of chance, dealers in produce from what should have been a sabbatical year, shepherds, tax-collectors and revenue supervisors.

Only slightly less despised, but not automatically unclean, were transport-workers, herdsmen, shopkeepers, physicians, butchers, goldsmiths, flax-combers, handmill cleaners, pedlars, weavers, barbers, launderers, blood-letters, bath attendants and tanners. There is a logic about each disapproval, given the original starting place. Borg, page 96.
3. Dunn, *Jesus' Call to Discipleship*, page 71.

tions made against him, but turned them into statements of positive intent. Here was what his message and ministry was all about, he said. Christ came to be *God's boundary-breaker* (to quote Dunn's evocative phrase).

What exactly was Jesus doing and saying?

First, he was not denying or deriding the idea of a People of God. How could he, when he came not to abolish but fulfil the divine scriptures on which the idea was based (Matthew 5:17)? What he broke wide open was the narrow identification of God's People by a few external observations, like the exact way in which Sabbath is observed or kosher food is preserved. Defilement is not a physical thing but an attitude of heart and mind. In Christ's own words:

> Don't you see that nothing that enters a man from the outside can make him 'unclean'—what comes out of a man is what makes him 'unclean'. For from within, out of men's hearts, come evil thoughts, sexual immorality, theft, murder, adultery, greed, malice, deceit, lewdness, envy, slander, arrogance and folly. All these evils come from inside and make a man 'unclean' (Mark 7:18-23).

Jesus did not abandon the vision of a People of God; he widened it and deepened it, by making the qualifications moral and spiritual.

Secondly, Jesus did not propose being 'soft on sin' (to quote a modern phrase). He called and enabled people to change their ways. In one of the most misquoted stories in the Bible, he did not say (as so often claimed), 'No-one has the right to condemn you; I certainly don't; forget it.' To the woman caught in adultery and enthusiastically condemned by some Pharisees (where was the man, by the way?), his actual words were 'Neither do I condemn you; go now and leave your life of sin' (John 8:1-11).

The theme is repeatedly underlined. Zacchaeus leaves his crooked tax-collecting and makes reparation. Mary Magdalene has the demons expelled. The leper is sent to register his cleansing with the religious authorities. The madman Legion is found clothed and sane. Mary of Bethany is invited, not *from* slavery at the kitchen sink but *to* learning at her rabbi's feet (one contemporary rabbi said he would rather teach a woman sexual immorality than let her pollute the *torah* by learning it).[4]

Not only come but eat

There is still the matter of the meals. Why specifically eat together? Another modern scholar suggests:

> ... his movement, with him at the centre, held festive meals in the villages they passed through, either in the open air or in the house of a sympathizer. A large number of his parables defended his practice of eating with outcasts. Indeed one may speculate that many of his parables may have been spoken in the context of these festive meals as the 'table talk' of Jesus.[5]

I think this is beyond doubt. The famous parable of the Great Banquet is a case in point. At just such a party,

---

4. Borg, page 146. See also the quote in the Mishnah: 'If any man teach his daughter the Torah, it is as though he taught her lechery' (Mishnah Sotah: 3, 4).
5. Borg, page 132.

responding to a kind of toast from an enthusiastic attender, Jesus launched into the humorous but searching story of the nobleman's great feast and the first-invited guests who turn him down with such ridiculous excuses. (What fun we have with 'I have married a wife and therefore I cannot come'!) The second invitation then goes out to 'the poor, the crippled, the blind and the lame', whilst to those who turned it down, 'none of you will get a taste' (Luke 14:15-24).

But there is more to it than that. The enthusiast at the party (in real life, not in the parable) shouts:

Blessed is the man who will eat
at the feast in the Kingdom of God.

Everyone knew what he meant. He was quoting one of the most attractive and famous prophetic songs of Isaiah, whose popularity in the time of Jesus is amply illustrated by many documents and prayers.

On this mountain the LORD Almighty will prepare
a feast of rich food for all peoples,
a banquet of aged wine -
the best of meats and the finest of wines....
The Sovereign LORD will wipe away the tears from all faces;
He will remove the disgrace ...
Let us rejoice and be glad in his salvation (Isaiah 25:6-9).

There can be no serious doubt that in his 'meals for all' Jesus was saying by implication what he elsewhere said directly—'Now is this scripture fulfilled before your eyes'. And in his parables he said it again, in powerful pictures.

Winning back the lost

This is the context of the greatest parable of all—the Prodigal Son. Why did he tell this scintillating tale? Luke explains:

> The Pharisees and the teachers of the law muttered, 'This man welcomes sinners and eats with them.'[6]

Jesus ripostes with two short stories, each marked by celebration over something lost and found. The successful shepherd invites his neighbours to the equivalent of drinks all round. The housewife finds her missing coin (part of her wedding ring) and has the girls in for a tea party. Then comes the powerful story of the foolish son whose lifestyle leads him to famine in a far country. Every detail in the story underlines how revoltingly 'unclean' and 'outside' he has become (reaching the depths in his job as a herder of unclean swine).

What happens when he comes to his senses and trudges home repentant? He offers to work his way back into family status. But his father shocks the community (who share the shame and insult of the boy's behaviour and will have organised a *qasasah* ceremony to declare him 'dead') by warmly welcoming him back. He celebrates with a feast, slaughtering a calf to provide enough food for the whole village. Meanwhile the elder son, stern and dutiful, refuses to join the meal. The story has come full circle. The self-righteous son has joined the Pharisees outside, whose criticism had sparked off the story. The unworthy son is eating and drinking inside with music and dancing. The whole definition of 'inside' and 'outside' has been reversed.

---

6. See the whole of Luke 15.

Christian separatism

What are the implications for Christians today? The church has failed repeatedly to follow its Lord in this matter. Recurring movements of evangelical renewal first rediscover the meaning of grace and then emulate Jesus in reaching out to the people beyond the pale. It still happens. New Christian movements in our time have pioneered work amongst the homeless, the drug addicts, the AIDS victims, the unemployed. Evangelism in prisons is another striking contemporary example. But each in turn sinks within a generation into the same kind of respectable externalism *that defines the people of God as those who belong to our party*. The identifying marks may be membership of a sect, assent to a particular doctrinal statement, promotion of a view of prophecy, exercise of a particular gift, acceptance of a certain style of leadership, observation of a subculture, or avoidance of a particular vice. Most subtle of all is the ever-recurring tendency to restrict membership of God's true church to those who can clearly explain the meaning of grace—which thus in turn becomes a meritorious label!

The test-question today will not be 'Is your food kosher?' (although I know some Hebrew Christian believers who get close to that). In some churches it could be 'Are you black or white?' It may well be 'Are you a Calvinist?' or perhaps 'Do you believe in the Millennium?' I know some churches where the vital question is 'Do you have a letter?' The crucial question may be more behaviour-based—Do you drink alcohol, Are you divorced, Do you speak in tongues? I know people condemned as total outsiders or welcomed as total insiders purely on the basis of their hymn book preference, their favoured musical instrument or their choice of network leader.

I myself have had the interesting experience of being banned from various pulpits for my views of women's leadership (in fact misquoted), my attitude to Roman Catholics (in fact misunderstood) and my approach to spiritual gifts (in fact misheard; I had said the opposite to what I was 'heard' to have said, as a live recording proved).

None of this surprises me, since I find the early church struggling with similar issues, in spite of Jesus' express words and example. But it saddens me (sometimes drives me close to despair) for it hinders the cause of evangelism and confuses the message of the evangelist.

In the eighteenth century, racked as it was by sectarianism and dissent, a large-hearted, Christ-loving leader brought these issues back into perspective in one of his hymns.

'What think ye of Christ?' is the test
    That tries both your state and your scheme
You cannot be right in the rest
    Until you are right about him.

It is no coincidence that he wrote a more famous hymn that begins:

Amazing grace, how sweet the sound
    That saved a wretch like me;
I once was lost but now I'm found,
    Was blind, but now I see.

Astonished appreciation of the grace of God in Christ which sent him to welcome outcasts and offer his life for them —this is what brings the Christian to follow his or her Lord in the dangerous, sensitive work of barrier-breaking. And this message of grace (a God who loves people simply because he is God and they are people) lies at the heart of the gospel of Christ.

Chapter 4

The Man who Mended People

Jesus made people whole. It was one of the most obvious things about him. He preached good news to the poor, announced release to captives, mended broken bodies and delivered the demonised. His own broken-ness on the cross of torment became the mending message and the symbol of *salvation*. Indeed, that very word 'salvation' (Greek, *soteria*) can equally be translated as healing, rescue, forgiveness or renewal.

Through his ministry of word and deed, supernatural power was released into the lives of despairing people. Apart from the events of the final week, two-thirds of Mark's Gospel are concerned with Christ's miraculous power. In the opinion of one serious modern scholar, 'to his contemporaries, it was the most significant thing about him'.[1]

That evening after sunset the people brought to Jesus all the sick and demon-possessed. The whole town gathered at the door, and Jesus healed many ... (Mark 1:32-34).

News about him spread all over Syria and people brought to him all who were ill .... Large crowds from Galilee, the

---

1. Borg, page 60.

Decapolis, Jerusalem, Judea and the region across the Jordan followed him (Matthew 4:24-25).

It was this that gave him a reputation that drew people to enquire more deeply. 'We know you are a teacher who has come from God. For no-one could perform the miraculous signs you are doing if God were not with him'; so said a religious leader in his night-time discussion with the 'Rabbi' (John 3:1-2). This was before the famous Galilee ministry had begun.

As well as referring to mass healings, the Gospel writers give detailed descriptions of fourteen ailments individually healed. These included fever, leprosy, paralysis, a withered hand, a bent back, internal haemorrhage, a deaf-and-dumb condition, blindness, dropsy, a severed ear, a 'sickness near death'. These all appear, sometimes more than once, in the Synoptic Gospels. John's account adds an official's son near death, an invalid for thirty-eight years, and a man blind from birth.

As well as these healings, there are three examples of people restored after death: nicely spread between a girl only just expired, a young man dead for something less than a day, and an adult buried for four days.[2]

Added to this are general references to and some detailed descriptions of 'exorcism'. That precise word is never used.

---

2. The individual healings are (in the Synoptic Gospels): Mark 1:29-31; 1:40-45; 2:1-17; 3:1-6; Luke 13:10-17; Mark 5:24-34; Mark 7:31-37; Mark 8:22-26; Luke 14:1-6; Luke 22:51; Luke 7:1-10 (most of them described by more than one writer). John adds 4:43-54; 5:1-15; 9. The three examples of people raised from death are in Mark 5:35-43; Luke 7:11-17; John 11.

Nor is the word 'possessed'. People were literally 'demonised'. The demons were dismissed and fled at the word of Christ. But what are we to make of all this in our modern scientific age when (we are assured) miracles cannot happen? First, let me pose a few suggested possibilities only to dismiss them.

Man without miracles?

Christ's miracles simply cannot be separated from his ministry. We cannot dismiss the first as mere wonder-stories from a credulous age and concentrate on the second, as if Jesus' teaching somehow stands on its own within no context of life and action. Separation of the two is physically impossible, psychologically absurd and spiritually fatal. It also makes nonsense of the Bible. Either we know that Jesus healed the sick or we know nothing about him. Biblical writers, contemporary historians, church memories and hostile criticism alike combine in telling us that he did these things. They give different opinions on why and how he did them, but they all agree that he did them. A non-miraculous Jesus is simply a figment of modern imagination: there is no evidence that such an anaemic figure even existed.

Myth without fact?

An exercise dauntingly described as 'demythologising' is one suggested solution. Pioneered by Rudolf Bultmann (1884-1976), the idea is to replace the language of a pre-scientific world view with ideas more conducive to modern mind-sets. No longer can we believe in a three-decker universe, with heaven above, hell below and earth between (each influencing the others with supernatural intrusions). Ideas like the Son of God 'coming down to earth' must therefore be dismissed. Powers from 'up there' at work through Jesus are likewise unacceptable.

Instead (it is proposed) we must disentangle the essential message from its mythological wrappings. The feeding of the five thousand we can see as a symbol of Christ's ability to satisfy human longings. Jesus walking on the water is a picture of the church tossed on the waves of circumstance and danger, but calmed by the presence of God. The healing miracles can be similarly treated. Sight for a blind man speaks to us of spiritual illumination. Healing of the lame symbolises strength to walk in ways that please God. Healing of the leper speaks of the sense of internal cleansing.

All very moving as far as it goes—and not unlike the way that Bible-believing preachers have 'spiritualised' the Jesus-stories throughout the centuries. But there is a difference. The spiritualiser believes that the thing actually happened. He or she reasons from the outer event to the inner meaning. But the demythologiser thinks it never happened. He reasons backwards. He proceeds from an accepted truth to a non-event. The first Christians believed in forgiveness so they told stories about cleansed lepers—and so on. But *why* did they believe in forgiveness (and moral strength and spiritual illumination and, for that matter, resurrection)? They tell us why. Because they were witnesses of these things—or they believed others who said *they* were witnesses of these things.[3]

Reverse the question. If most of the stories about Jesus are not factual, what about him is factual? What reason is there to believe anything whatever about him?

---

3. John 20:30-31; 21:24-25; 2 Peter 1:16-18. Ironically, Peter uses the word 'myth' (invented story) to describe what the typical Gospel narrative is *not*. He even quotes the event most likely to be dismissed as mythological (the transfiguration) and insists 'we were eyewitnesses'.

Rabbi or Hassid?

Another approach has proved attractive in recent years. Its motivation is credible. It has the merit of taking history seriously. It does not give a complete answer, but it deserves attention. It helps us to understand how Jesus was 'seen' in his time and historical context.

Study of ancient Jewish tradition suggests that Jesus can be more readily compared to the first-century Galilean Hassidim (holy men) than to the Jerusalem Rabbis.[4] Some examples of these men of spiritual power make fascinating reading. Josephus describes one Eleazar, roughly contemporary with Jesus. The Talmud refers to others, like Hanina ben Dosa and Honi the Circle-Drawer. Several shrines in today's Galilee recall others.[5]

'Charismatic Hassidim' is the label that modern scholars have given them. They were people acutely aware of the living God. They spent much time in private prayer and personal, direct communion with him. To many they presented a more impressive picture than the pragmatic and worldly priests. To Galileans they offered a more attractive image than the rather legalistic rabbis. They had a reputation for healing prayers, they practised exorcism, and at least one seemed to specialise in praying for rain during times of drought.

The reader who knows his Bible will already have thought of the biblical action-prophets like Elijah and Elisha—and it is to exactly that precedent that the holy men appealed.[6] There is an increasing willingness on the part of modern Jewish

4. Vermes, chapter 3, pages 58-82; Borg, chapter 4.
5. Josephus, *Antiquities* 8:46-48.
6. Elijah's ministry (1 Kings 17-19); Elisha's ministry (2 Kings 2-8). Jesus himself drew attention to the likeness: Luke 4:24-27.

scholars to recognise Jesus of Nazareth as one, perhaps the greatest, of that line of action-prophets or men of power. The Gospel record implies that some people had the same idea at the time (Matthew 16:13-16).

The likenesses to Jesus are intriguing, but they should not be exaggerated. As with the Teachers of the Torah, so with the Men of Power, Jesus offered more differences than resemblances.

The Hassidim had no message of the Kingdom-come. They lived solitary lives of asceticism, and drew people, not to follow them, but simply to benefit from their prayers. They neither claimed to be, nor were thought to be, Messiahs. They concentrated on private devotion, not public teaching. Jesus' treatment of demonised people was markedly different from theirs. *They* used incantations, elaborate ceremonies, herbs (swallowed or inhaled), the recital of famous biblical names, and the proclamation of God's titles. *He* exercised authority, speaking the word of command at which the dark powers fled. The awed spectators quickly noticed the difference. Significantly they attributed his acts of power to his authoritative teaching, 'What is this? A new teaching—and with authority! He even gives orders to evil spirits and they obey him' (Mark 1:23-27).

To say that Jesus was in a different category to these sincere healers is not to denigrate them in the least. There have been others like them before and since in Jewish experience. Christian history has its close parallels. One thinks of Columba, Aidan and the great Celtic missionaries who took the gospel from Ireland to Scotland and thence to northern England. Later centuries produced characters like Francis of Assisi, Teresa of Avila, some of the early Anabaptists and more recently the Pentecostalist pioneers of the early twentieth century. They knew much of the immediacy of faith and the inflow and outflow of the Holy Spirit. But Jesus was the *giver* of the Holy Spirit, the divine Son who only and always did those things that pleased his Father. Observers asked in astonishment, 'What kind of man is this?' He gave the staggering explanation that as God continually works, keeping his created universe in being, so the Son constantly works in healing and redemption (Mark 4:41; John 5:16-18).

The Reason Why

How then should we regard Jesus the Healer? How essential to his message were his miracles? How do we approach them today—as one-off signs to admire, or as examples to emulate and models to follow?

First we must ask, why did he do it? The question may sound simple, but the answer leads along several paths.

1. *Declarations of Love*

Jesus healed people because he cared about them. Often we read he was 'moved with compassion' at their plight.[7] In his human actions he focused that divine characteristic which his own Bible affirmed to be one of God's greatest attributes. The Hebrew word is *chesed*—unfailing mercy and steadfast love.

God was moved with pity at the groans of Israelite slaves in Egypt. God's compassion pleaded through lawgivers and prophets for the weary, the weak and the widow. That same God was seen in Jesus, reaching out in healing, and delivering love. 'God is like this,' said Jesus, by healing the sick.[8]

---

7. The compassion of Christ: Matthew 9:35-38; 11:28-30; Mark 1:40-42.
8. 'God is like this': Exodus 6:5-6; Psalm 91:1-8; 103; Isaiah 58; 61:1-2.

2. *Demonstrations of Power*

Christ's actions often produced awe and amazement. They displayed love-with-power, and 'authority' which is power-under-control.

> The people all tried to touch him, because power was coming from him and healing them all (Luke 6:19 cf. Mark 2:12).

However, Jesus himself set little store by amazement as a route to faith. He consistently refused to 'perform' simply to impress; dismissing such requests as signs of a 'wicked and adulterous generation asking for miracles'. His attitude was consistent with that of his Jewish Bible which warned that supernatural power was not invariably from God; the test was, did it promote Truth?[9] The idea that he performed miracles to draw attention to himself is directly contradicted by the fact that he often pledged the recipients to secrecy.[10]

3. *Signposts to identity*

He sometimes appealed to his miracles as evidence of his identity as Son of God.

> The very work that the Father has given me to finish, and which I am doing, testifies that the Father has sent me (John 5:36).

But in these cases, it was not the wonder of his works that was

---

9. Signs and wonders tested by truth: Deuteronomy 13:1-5; John 6:24-29; 2 Thessalonians 2:1-12 (especially verse 9).
10. The 'secrecy' of Jesus: Matthew 8:1-4; Mark 5:35-43; 8:27-30.

the main point, as if something eternal was achieved by making people gasp. The sign-value of Christ's healings was more to do with the identity of those he healed than the precise nature of the sickness tackled. Lepers were banned from human intercourse in home and synagogue. The demon-possessed were feared and shunned. The physically handi-capped were excluded from priestly service. By healing such people, Jesus brought them back into the worshipping com-munity and affirmed them as God's children. The principle was essentially the same as that of 'eating with sinners'.

4. *Announcing the Kingdom*

The element of 'power and authority' in the miracles was designed to express God's kingdom-intervention. 'If I drive out demons by the finger of God, then the kingdom of God has come to you,' he announced (Luke 11:20). When he sent out his apostles in turn, it was with a kingdom programme that declared the same terms, demonstrated with the same actions (Luke 9:1-2).

The 'message' of the miracles was identical to that of the preaching. Both announced that God had intervened to fulfil his ancient promise. 'Some day' had become 'now'. God was establishing his reign and rule in human hearts. Jesus' life, work and teaching personified that kingdom, for in his heart and life God's will was perfectly done. His conflict with Satan in the wilderness and subsequent expulsion of demons, de-clared his victory over the powers of darkness. At the cross and the empty tomb he delivered the decisive blow. Now, by new birth, that kingdom comes to believing hearts. Christians are 'rescued from the dominion of darkness and brought ... into the kingdom of the Son he loves' (Colossians 1:13).

The kingdom of God is creation healed. Christ's healings and exorcisms were signs and symbols of that ultimate healing. The cross is the price fully paid for it. The Return of Christ will see its consummation.[11]

Healing today?

Now a question: is the healing ministry of Jesus an example to admire or a command to follow? Are his miracles simply signs that point to a unique Saviour at work during one short period of history? Or do they constitute a command to 'go and do likewise' in his power and by his Spirit?

Evangelical Christians hold several different opinions on the matter, whilst all agreeing on the facts of the biblical miracles.

Those of 'Reformed' persuasion underline the element of *uniqueness*. Christ was the only Son of the Father, and he accordingly did what no other can expect to do. The healing ministry, to them, constitutes God's stamp of approval of that one incomparable person. It also points to the deepest implications of his saving gospel. They quote Peter's words on the day of Pentecost:

Men of Israel, listen to this: Jesus of Nazareth was a man accredited by God to you by miracles, wonders and signs, which God did among you through him' (Acts 2:22).

---

11. The kingdom of God: Daniel 7:13-14; Luke 1:31-33; Matthew 12:28; Luke 17:21; John 3:3-7; Colossians 1:13. See Bridge, *Power Evangelism and the Word of God* Part 3. In the Gospels, 75 references to the kingdom speak of God's offer and invitation; 20 references describe the changed lives of the kingdom's subjects.

At most, this approach finds an extension of that love-power-sign ministry only in the actions of Christ's immediate heralds and apostles. For the rest of us, there is encouragement towards faith as *submission to God's sovereign will*, rather than as a means to obtain a longed-for goal. This view certainly encourages us to pray for ourselves and for others, but Calvinists always emphasise that the highest prayer is 'Thy will be done'. Surely they are right: it was *his* highest prayer.

Finally, this approach sees the ongoing works of medicine, education, social welfare, pastoral care, counselling and research as reflections and reminders of Christ's compassion and God's 'general grace'—especially when performed by churches and individual Christians. These are not 'miraculous'—but they are examples of God at work.

Charismatic Christians, to varying degrees, make the connection more direct. They focus on the present experience of Christ in us and with us, by his Spirit. If Jesus is indeed 'the same yesterday and today and forever' (Hebrews 13:8), surely we should see him doing the same things, through his committed followers?

Some Charismatics strongly associate healing with 'faith' (either in the one who prays or the one for whom prayer is made). By faith they mean strong expectancy that the healing will indeed be granted.

Understandably, and predictably, this approach has two equal and opposite outcomes. Remarkable healings are sometimes seen; of that there can be no doubt, even when we make full allowance for exaggeration, autosuggestion, the psychosomatic element, and so on. But more are unhealed than healed. That too is irrefutable. And the unhealed can be left

with crippling problems of guilt, self-blame, doubt or disillusionment.

Mainline Pentecostalists have from their beginnings exercised a distinctive healing ministry. Like the later Charismatics, they draw attention to the varied 'spiritual gifts' described
at work in the early church. These included words of knowledge, gifts of healing and discerning of spirits (1 Corinthians
12:4-11). By this means, they suggest, the living Christ still
continues his healing and delivering ministry through his
body, the supernaturally-equipped church. Certain people are
gifted with regular healing ministries. Others may have the
occasional experience.

Pentecostalists also have a distinctive *doctrine* of healing.
They draw attention to Matthew's comments on Jesus' Galilee ministry. He links the healings with the 'Servant of the
Lord' passages in Isaiah, and especially the phrase translated
somewhat elastically as 'He took up our infirmities and
carried our diseases'. But elsewhere in the New Testament
(they point out), 'Servant' passages are applied to Jesus'
atoning death upon the cross, where:

> He was pierced for our transgressions and crushed for
> our iniquities; the punishment that brought us peace was
> upon him, and by his wounds we were healed.

Pentecostalists reason that if this is so, then healing of
sickness is 'in the atonement' as surely as is forgiveness of
sins. In both cases, all that is needed is repentance and faith.[12]

---

12. Isaiah's servant-pictures and their fulfilment in Jesus: Isaiah 42:1-
4; 49:1-7; 50:4-10; 52:13-15; 53; Matthew 8:16-17; 12:15-21.

The reasoning, I suggest, is attractive but flawed. It is difficult to attach any real meaning to a concept of Christ 'carrying our sicknesses on the cross' in the sense that he undoubtedly carried our sins. The outworking is certainly not comparable. Everyone who repents and believes is certainly forgiven; manifestly not everyone is physically healed (although some are).

Consistent with his regular method of writing, Matthew lovingly and joyfully recognises an illustration and promise of his Master's healing ministry in Isaiah's great picture. But it is a picture of Christ's life in Galilee, not his crucifixion in Jerusalem.

Third Wave Christians (to coin a well-used phrase) lay much stress on *the sign value* of healing and deliverance. Christ's words and deeds heralded the Kingdom of God, announcing his saving intervention and his transforming rule. Since the message of the Kingdom is now given to us, we should expect to see similar confirmation. Indeed, teachers like John Wimber and Bishop David Pytches suggest that Christians today may learn from Jesus the principles and methods needed. How may we recognise evil spirits at work? How may we encourage expectancy for healing? We should learn from him just as his first disciples learned—and put what we learn into practice as they did.[13]

Again there are difficulties here about message and method. Is our kingdom message today precisely the same as theirs in the first century, since the heart of it was *Jesus visibly and physically present*? Do today's answers to prayer really bear

13. See Wimber, *Power Evangelism* and *Power Healing*; Pytches, *Come Holy Spirit*.

comparison with Christ's miracles of power? Actual hard
evidence of the outworking is hard to come by, and when
offered is somewhat opaque. Certainly some are healed.
Certainly many are helped. Certainly demons are sometimes
cast out. Certainly the offer of the gospel and the planting of
new churches is sometimes furthered by a 'signs-and-won-
ders' ministry (strikingly so in some third world countries).
But whilst gratitude and worship are appropriate in response
to any and every work of mercy, it is hard to equate seriously
these answers to prayer with the miracles of Jesus himself.
Those, as Christian doctors often point out, were always
immediate, complete and permanent.

To their credit, Third Wave enthusiasts have challenged
the materialistic, secular, closed-system thinking which many
Western Christians have imbibed from a godless society.
Miracles embarrass us. The supernatural makes us uncom-
fortable. More liberal churchmen get around it by 'demythologising' the Gospel accounts. Evangelicals do something
similar when they 'dispensationalise' them; committing them
to a past period in God's purposes, aimed at someone else.
Many Christians need to experience what John Wimber
describes as a paradigm shift, and become at least more open
to the possibility of the supernatural.

Does Jesus work today?
All true Christians can surely agree on some points. Our
Saviour really did those things. By them he declared his
identity, his gospel and his kingdom. We are called today to
declare those three great truths, through our corporate life, our
evangelism, our compassionate concern and our personal
lifestyles. This is why the Christian church has always been

at the forefront of medicine, education, social care, the search for justice, and everything that makes life more bearable, more human, and more in line with that original creation as it was before sin polluted and marred it.

The growing tendency of Evangelicals to put 'care' and 'mission' side by side seems to me to be wholly admirable and genuinely reflective of Christ's ministry then and now. It is in fact a return to the older Evangelicalism, from which many had drifted in a reaction against the corroding influence of the so-called 'Social Gospel', which was something quite different.[14]

The church has a message that can bring people to God, nurture them in a community of forgiven and forgiving people, and steer them towards maturity in Christ at every level of their lives. That, surely, spells 'healing' in the widest and deepest sense of the word.

---

14. 'Social Gospel' was the name widely used early this century to describe a liberal Christian approach which virtually equated the search for what we now call 'human rights' with the coming of the kingdom of God. Preachers of the social gospel almost completely abandoned the idea of divine revelation and what they called 'personal conversion'. *Some* forms of modern 'Liberation Theology' do the same today.

Chapter 5

The Man who Made Disciples

Modern churches make converts; Jesus made disciples. This is one of the most striking differences between his method and ours. It is not merely a matter of semantics.

The word 'disciple' (*mathetos*) appears 269 times in the New Testament. Usually, though not always, it describes those who attached themselves to Jesus during his public ministry. There were probably a few hundred at most. It was also the most natural thing for Christians to call themselves after the birth of the church. Indeed, 'Christian' was at first simply a nickname for 'disciple' (Acts 11:26).

Another self-chosen name was 'Followers of the Way'; we might translate it 'Way Folk'. This was a description they shared with disciples of John the Baptist and, we now realise, with members of the Essene movement, of which the Qumran scrolls have taught us so much. All these groups were drawing on the great call of Isaiah to prepare a way for the Lord; a highway for God's saving action.[1]

The word 'disciple' means literally a learner or a listener. It was used to describe someone willing to give some philoso-

---

1. Preparing a Way for the Lord: Isaiah 40:1-3; Matthew 3:1-3; Luke 3:1-14. Notice Paul's words 'I persecuted the followers of this Way to their death' (Acts 22:1-5). For Essenes, see Vermes, pages 26, 220-1, 223.

phy a careful hearing. It was also used to describe medical students and craft apprentices. In Jewish religious circles it implied serious commitment to some rabbi or sect.

Significantly, Jesus' last commission to his disciples was to 'make disciples, teaching them to obey everything I have commanded'. Significantly too, the commission was accompanied by a claim to authority (Matthew 28:18-20).

The gospel is the good news that the Son of God brings authority into people's lives, teaching them to follow in his way. This is possible because he has put out of the way all that once kept us estranged from God.

The Pharisees, too, had their disciples—about six thousand of them in Jesus' time, according to Josephus. The Pharisee teachers were called 'rabbis'; at that time the word simply meant 'teacher', and only later became an honorific title, like 'Very Reverend'.

The rabbis' system of training disciples offers thought-provoking comparison with that of Jesus. There are striking resemblances but even more striking differences.[2]

A rabbi was usually a married family man. His disciples came to him and asked for instruction; he did not 'call' them. Somewhere between eight and fifteen of them might be a suitable number. Sometimes disciples left their secular work for a limited period to devote every hour to instruction. For that period they would live at the rabbi's house (his *beyt*, it was called: the word implied both house and school). They would take turns to minister to the rabbi's personal domestic needs: a process that benefited both ways, as they in turn received his conversational 'table-talk'.

2. For information about Pharisees, see Borg, pages 88-96, and Stallings, chapters 1 and 7.

The rabbi's aim was to encourage his pupils to memorise and apply the Torah (the Law of Moses, especially the book of Leviticus). They discussed its meaning and explored its detailed application to their 'modern life', so different from the desert context of the original. To this end they quoted hundreds of discussions, comments and precedents from other rabbis and scholars. To promote debate, the teacher would use considerable skills in repartee, argument, storytelling, analogy and folk-wisdom, as well as proposing hypothetical situations and problems to solve. This wealth of material, roughly classified as *halakah* (lifestyle) and *haggadah* (story) was eventually reduced to writing in the maze-like Mishnah and the later even more complex Talmud. It corresponds roughly to what Jesus called 'the tradition of the fathers', which he sometimes quoted with approval and sometimes severely criticised.[3]

A rabbi attached great importance to the spoken word. This was regarded as superior to the merely written-and-read word because it came through the personality of the speaker in the 'living' context of discussion and exploration. It was, in short, more immediate than a book. Teaching made much use of facial expression, accent, intonation, gestures and anecdotes.

---

3. Jesus' use and criticism of 'tradition': Matthew 5:17-48; 7:1-5; 15:1-20; 19:1-12; Mark 7, especially verses 8, 13. For Jesus' 'approval' of rabbinical traditions, cf. Sermon on the Mount and the Lord's Prayer, many of whose phrases reflect the concerns and priorities of the rabbis. See for example Christ's teaching on divorce which contradicts the school of Hillel and favours the school of Shammai (Matthew 19:3-12). More often the choice was in reverse, Hillel being less rigid about outward observance in contrast to motive, and to that extent more 'like Jesus'. See also *Tishrei* Magazine, Vol 2, No 1, Spring 1994.

The colourful Aramaic language with its natural rhyming and rhythm acted as a vivid counterpoint to the more formal and 'religious' Hebrew in which the scriptures were quoted. The material was taught in a kind of half-chant called 'cantillation'.[4]

Great emphasis was laid on memorisation, which could be amazingly efficient. A modern scholar describes the whole process as 'a highly structured, refined and formalised technique that passed on information with extraordinary accuracy'.[5]

A rabbi would often employ two or three extra-close disciples who were admitted to the most intimate moments (although one is recorded as complaining that secret observation of his lovemaking with his wife was going a little too far!). The task of these closest disciples (called *tana-im*) was to memo- rise huge tracts of the rabbi's own teaching, and in turn din it into the memories of the others. In spite of the preference for 'live speech' they were encouraged to make written notes or memoirs. Were Peter, James and John Christ's equivalents of these tana-im? And could such written notes have formed the basis of the Gospel records, which Papias and others in the early church referred to as 'apostles' memoirs'?

Orthodox rabbis rarely travelled far. Disciples came to them, and took the initiative in applying. They studied, or even lived, together in their 'school' or 'house'. The word 'house' referred both to the living group and to the building in which they met—usually the rabbi's own home. In Jesus' case the beyt was the house often referred to in Mark's Gospel, and variously described as 'his (Jesus') home', 'Peter's house', 'the house of Peter's mother-in-law' or most often simply 'the house' or 'home'.[6]

---

4. Wilder, pages 18-26. 5. Stallings, chapter 7, 'The School of Jesus'.
6. Jesus' House in Mark's Gospel: 1:29-34; 2:1-2; 6:1, 30.

This was in Capernaum (literally the village of Nahum) on the northwest coast of Lake Galilee. The ruins of the house can still be seen today, a hundred yards from the synagogue that also features in several Gospel accounts. The house is identified by the succession of church buildings unfortunately erected successively on top of it. But at least they serve to pinpoint and preserve what must be one of the best-authenticated 'holy sites' in modern Israel.

The rooms are built rather haphazardly around a more or less central courtyard. Shortly after Jesus' time two larger rooms were knocked into one to form one of the earliest *dominus ecclesiae* (house-churches) in Christendom. Excavating Franciscans early in the twentieth century found fallen plaster from the walls clearly inscribed with Christian signs and graffiti. The name Jesus is scratched on several pieces.

Resemblances between Jesus' discipling and that of the rabbis are obvious. The basic principle of personal tutoring, the choice of a small group, the shared home, the master-pupil relationship—all are similar. The likeness extends to the method of teaching. Rabbis loved stories, similes and anecdotes, although none of these reached the brilliance of Christ's parables, which are totally unique. His teaching too can be divided roughly into the halachic and the haggadic, the lifestyle instruction and the narrative story.

Their starting place was the same, too. Jesus took completely for granted the great Mosaic and prophetic themes. The one holy God, his sovereign love, his will expressed in commandments, his love displayed in rescuing the enslaved, his call to Israel to be a light to the world—all is assumed, illustrated and explored. But startlingly new was his message of the kingdom and his welcome of the wanderer. This was also expressed in the simple fact that he did not merely receive disciples; he went out and found them. Andrew the fisherman, Levi the tax-man, Simon the radical politician, Nathanael the mystic; these people did not find their Rabbi; he found them and uttered the crisp command, 'Follow me'.

The same message of a seeking Saviour was expressed in Christ's tireless missionary journeys. They took him extraordinary distances into today's Syria, Lebanon, Jordan, Samaria and Judaea, as well as all over the province of Galilee. Then in turn he sent out his disciples on similar missions— first six pairs and then another seventy-two in pairs, making seven times twelve in all. To Jewish ears this would convey obvious symbolic meaning. *Twelve* would represent the tribes of Israel. Rabbis spoke of *seven* pagan nations of the world (because of the seven commandments given to Noah after the flood, according to their tradition). *Pairs* symbolised reliable witness, as in Matthew 18:16 quoting Deuteronomy 19:15. On these journeys they followed his own pattern of action: 'drive out demons, cure diseases, preach the kingdom'.[7]

Totally new, too, was the unprecedented place given to women, at a time when they had little or no place in religious life, prayed separately from men (if at all) and were not taught the scriptures. Before marriage they were secluded, and after marriage could only go out in public if veiled. Conversation with men outside their family circle was forbidden. No respectable man, let alone a rabbi, would converse with a female stranger. Their evidence in court was considered valueless.

Seen against that background, Jesus' approach was astonishing, even shocking. His immediate circle of travelling

7. Jesus sends out his disciples: Luke 9:1-6; 10:1-20.

helpers included women. Mary Magdalene was one of his closest disciples, and privileged with other women to be the first witnesses of the resurrection. Several wealthy women gave financial support to the travelling team. The sight of this large group of disciples, male and female, travelling with a holy man and rabbi must have been sensational, especially if accompanied also by the newly-healed, the newly-exorcised and the newly-converted.[8]

Life in the early church, as expressed in Acts and Epistles, reflected much of the disciple-making ministry of Jesus. The rhythmical rote-words from the Last Supper and the Lord's Prayer are exactly the kind of thing that disciple-teaching specialised in. When Paul reports what he has 'received' and now 'passed on' (even to Gentile churches) he is using technical discipleship terms; he was discipled, and now he disciples. Again there is the rhythmical easily-memorised phraseology.[9] Paul also employed the rabbi-disciple pattern in evangelism.

---

8. Jesus' attitude to women: Mark 14:1-9; Luke 7:36-50; 8:1-3; 10:38-42; John 4:7-30. The women who supported his group financially are listed as Mary Magdalene, Mary the mother of James, and Salome (Mark 15:40-41). These women had followed him in Galilee and cared for his needs. Many other women had come up with him to Jerusalem (Matthew 27:55-56). See Borg, pages 133-5.

It is only fair to say that the Mishnah also records some much less negative views of women, and that in comparison with the Gentile world of Christ's day, the Jews accorded a high and honouring place to women within the privacy of the family.

9. Memorised and rhyming formulae in the early church: 1 Corinthians 11:23-26; 15:3-5; Matthew 28:18-20. See also the many 'faithful sayings' in letters to Timothy and Titus.

Our gospel came not only with words but with power - You know how we lived among you - You became imitators of us and of the Lord - You became a model to all believers - the Lord's message rang out from you (1 Thessalonians 1:5-8).

James' letter is full of direct and indirect references to the remembered teaching, paraphrasing the words rather than repeating them with wooden literalism. Today we call it dynamic equivalence. In those days it was the rabbinical method of discipling, involving exact memorising and paraphrased application; both strengthened by observation of shared lifestyle (notice how intensely practical is James' teaching).

A method for today?

'Discipling'—the making of disciples—has become a warm issue in evangelical churches. There are several reasons for this healthy return to the method of Jesus.

Mass evangelism, though owned and blessed by God for its clear gospel call, has left many casualties and half-born or half-grown Christians. The old concept of 'Follow-up' had its virtues, but failed to grasp the nettle, with its concept of voluntary classes and 'a church of your choice'. The more scriptural concept of 'Nurture', introduced (as far as I recall) in the 1984 Mission England, propelled churches closer to the discipling model. So, too, did a move away from 'sudden conversion' viewed as the most satisfactory model for evangelism.

In fact, experience declares it to be the least satisfactory. The imagined virtues of the 'name-the-moment-and-mark-the-spot' kind of experience have produced an evangelical mythology in which the preferred route is the Damascus Road type. The myth has been enlarged by oversimplified caricatures of John Wesley's, John Bunyan's, Martin Luther's and St Augustine's conversions. In fact, not one of their experiences was half as sudden and instantly complete as we like to think. And has anyone tried to work out the day on which the apostle Peter was born again?

A pagan society has compelled a radical rethink about conversion and discipleship. Perhaps it was once sufficient to teach enquirers 'the Way of Salvation' one week, 'the Way of Assurance' the next, then supply them with a brief list of do's and don'ts, and introduce them as new church members. Perhaps, though I doubt it! But certainly not now. The average newly-declared Christian throughout the western world, as well as in Britain, emerges from an almost totally pagan background. Ideas about God will be grotesquely inaccurate. The Bible will be an unknown book. Christian morality will be unexplored territory. Some forbidden occult influence will be common, and some blatantly immoral entanglement almost inevitable. Paul's 'such were some of you' is back with us; we live in today's Corinth (1 Corinthians 6:9-11).

People have been systematically, if subliminally, trained in godless, amoral and secular thinking, through a diet of advertising, education, entertainment and media activity. They need to be retrained in right thinking and right behaviour, which will involve challenging practically every presupposition of today's society.

The new churches

Originally known as house-churches, these vibrant new expressions of Christian zeal have also brought discipling back on to the agenda. Reacting against the excessive individualism and pseudo-democracy of older evangelicals, they have entertained radical experiments in disciplined living and interventionist leadership. Mistakes were almost inevitable, especially when most Christian history and tradition (with the lessons to be learned from it) was dismissed as irrelevant.

'Heavy shepherding', personality cults and manipulative methods have now been abandoned by most of the new church networks. Their still-radical, but now more balanced approach, has much to teach others.

A typical 'new church' will gather interested contacts through its big celebrations and its innovative witnessing, but garner the harvest in small-group activity. A 'basics' or 'foundation-course' for enquirers leads in turn to a deeper discipleship course, so that a year may well pass before the potential convert is ready for public commitment to Christ and his people. As likely as not, this will be followed by a further training course in service, witnessing and the exercise of gifts. Yet another series will prepare people for minor leadership roles—and equip them in turn to disciple others.

Older denominations have in turn learned from the newer, once the scandal and shock had abated, and the almost inevitable sheepstealing had run its course. *Youthwork* magazine, for example, launched a twelve-month discipleship course. Many Anglicans use *Saints Alive* and *Saints in Healing* with videos and workbooks, to produce first believers and then serving lay-workers. Baptists have long used extended courses leading to baptism and church membership.

The *Alpha Manual* is a course using cassettes and work-books, originally produced by Holy Trinity Church, Brompton, but now widely used inter-denominationally as a personal evangelism and discipling course, lasting fourteen weeks. The first title is *Who is Jesus?* and the final one (having examined the cross, faith, scripture, guidance, spiritual growth, witnessing and church life) is significantly labelled *How can I make the most of the rest of my life?* The course ends with a celebration meal, to which the participants invite non-Christian friends, witness to them, and then hopefully begin the process all over again with a new intake—another reflection of Jesus' method!

The much-debated Willow Creek Community Church in Chicago looks at first like an exercise in mass evangelism, with its 'presentations' slanted towards a completely uncommitted audience. A second look reveals that its real key is the two-year discipling course, into which attenders at the big events are recruited.[10]

The elements of discipleship
These are obvious by now, and only need to be summarised. There must be *listening and learning*. This requires time for questioning (both ways), for learning facts, and for receiving hands-on training. Mark's Gospel is full of this kind of discipling.

There must be *genuine relationship* between leader and led, teacher and pupils. Role models presented in an atmos-

---

10. See *Aware* magazine, Paternoster Publications, April-May 1994, for an excellent summary of the discipling issue past and present.

Alpha Manual is copyright with Holy Trinity Brompton, Brompton Road, London, SW7 1JA.

phere of trust are essential—exactly as Paul describes at Thessalonica (1 Thessalonians 1, 2). John's Gospel reveals much of this, both in personal interviews (chapters 1-7) and group dialogue (the upper room, chapters 13-17).

There must be *community life*. Disciples learn from each other, in mutual interface. Mark's Gospel shows how the first disciples learned from each other's mistakes. The mistakes were many and frustrating, but the Master persevered with them, as he does with us (1:35-39; 3:31-34; 4:10-20; 5:37-43; 7:17-23; 8:14-21; 9:28-37; 10:35-45).

Fourth, there is *commissioning and service*. This distinguished Jesus' method from that of the rabbis. They produced men with knowledge; he produced people with a mission and 'sent them out'. A near-fatal mistake (which this writer has made at times) is to teach, train, activate—and then give the new disciples nothing to do, because of lack of vision, pulpit domination, or over-rigid church structures. Having learned the lesson twenty years ago, I sometimes tease cautious-minded churches where some mystical concept of 'maturity' prevails. At the pace they function, a new disciple may be ready to give out hymn books at the door after twenty years training—as long as that makes him over forty-five!

The content of discipleship courses will vary according to circumstance and denomination. A certain minimum seems essential. This writer has used a twelve to fifteen-week course in several successive churches. To God's glory alone, it can be said that many hundreds have been converted and brought into membership. A few hundred have become committed witnesses and lay-workers. Scores, at least, have become leaders, pastors, or missionaries (short or long-term). Most of them originally 'came to church' because of its caring reputation, listened to systematic biblical preaching, and then joined small groups for enquirers and disciples.

Facts of the Faith

New Christians need to know the content of the gospel of the grace of God and the meaning of the cross. They need to know the basis of assurance. They need some grasp of the truth about God as Creator, Father and Redeemer. They must be taught the essentials of the life of Jesus, his manhood and his deity. They require some understanding—and experience—of the person and work of the Holy Spirit. They need some certainty about the authority and inspiration of scripture. They need some elementary grasp of Christian doctrine.

Practice of the Faith

The new Christian should be taught how to read the Bible to hear God's voice, and how to build a personal devotional life of prayer and meditation. The importance of public corporate worship needs to be explained. Whatever concept of sacraments, style of worship and system of leadership prevails must be explained: what seems obvious to the old-stager can be puzzling and difficult to the newcomer.

Christian morality needs to be taught carefully, including sexual morality, the importance of a servant-attitude and approaches to work, leisure and finance.

The building and preserving of relationships within the fellowship has to be learned and explored.

Passing on the Faith

New Christians should be taught how to witness effectively in their natural circle of friends, neighbours, workmates and family. Each true conversion expands a hitherto unreached circle of other potential converts. That is why the newest are often the most effective in personal evangelism. The disciple can be taught how to discover and exercise his particular gift, calling and role, in the church and in the world.

In none of this is the atmosphere of pulpit or lecture-hall appropriate. The whole dynamic of discipling requires relationships, interface, dialogue and exploration—just as it worked amongst the Twelve and their associates.

A daunting task

The example of Christ the truest Evangelist beckons us, however often we tire or fail. In the words of the *Aware* magazine already quoted:

> If at the end of your discipling course the 'disciple' files away his notes neatly and never refers to them again, you have failed. But if you have launched another human life in an unending pursuit of God, you have achieved your aim.

Is any lesser goal worthwhile, in the light of Calvary?

Chapter 6

The Man who Glimpsed the Future

Standing on the western slopes of the Mount of Olives is an awesome experience. Gethsemane and the Kedron valley nestle below. On the opposite slope is the city of Jerusalem, shimmering in its sunlit, golden limestone splendour. The first time I stood there I had a strange feeling of *deja vu*. Was this due to a long-remembered illustration from my first Children's Bible? What I had naively imagined in my infancy to be a photograph, pictured Jesus seated on these slopes as he uttered his lament over the city and warned of its fate, less than a week before his own death.[1]

That same childhood was scattered with preachers much given to speculation on 'the prophetic scriptures', and Olivet appeared frequently in the scenarios. I knew the valley between mount and city to be the legendary 'valley of decision' where the nations would gather for judgment. I knew of the great promise that the Lord's feet would stand 'in that day' upon the Mount of Olives. I had read and heard of the river emerging from beneath the altar and flowing down through Kedron to the Dead Sea, bringing cleansing and renewal wherever it flowed.[2]

1. Olivet discourse: Mark 13; Matthew 24 and Luke 21.
2. Joel 3:14; Zechariah 14:1-5; Ezekiel 47.

And what of those dark warnings uttered here, of armies surrounding the city and not one temple stone left upon another? Teenage reading of Dean Farrar's *Early Days of Christianity* familiarised me with those awful days of AD 70 when city and temple were put to sword and flame. But visiting preachers assured me that Farrar had got it wrong (what else would you expect from a liberal Anglican?) and the *real* fulfilment was yet to come—probably in my lifetime.[3]

Now, in my late forties, I sat on those slopes and recalled the excitement of 1948 when Israel became a sovereign state once more and many Jews returned from worldwide exile. 1967, too, when Israeli soldiers stormed down these slopes, fought their way through the alleys of the biblical city, and recaptured the retaining wall of the temple. Did this bring to an end (as some asserted) 'the times of the Gentiles' (Luke 21:24) of which Jesus spoke in this place?

In short, Olivet represented prophetic debate and fulfilment. For on its slopes the Man from Heaven peered into the future, and invited his followers to watch with him.

The tradition still has echoes on that hillside, amongst Jews, Arabs and oriental Christians. Burial on this mountain slope (half-covered now by white tombstones shining in the eastern sun) is much to be desired. The optimistic assumption is that those interred here will be 'first up' on the Day of Resurrection. Well forward in the queue when the Books are opened, they will thus be able to present their alibis early in the day, perhaps before the Judge becomes tired of the sameness of a million excuses. So the theory goes. Is that why Robert Maxwell was recently buried there?

---

3. *The Early Days of Christianity* by Dean F W Farrar.

Certainly Christ's words solemnly uttered here contained dire warnings of the future. In what is often called the Little Apocalypse (Mark 13) he clearly spoke of the coming destruction of Jerusalem by the Romans, and connected that catastrophe with the city's failure to recognise its day of opportunity. Asked by his startled followers to expand on this, he did so in words that have become part of Christian prophetic vocabulary.

Watch out that no-one deceives you

When you hear of wars and rumours of wars

Nation will rise against nation

There will be earthquakes and famines

You will be handed over and flogged

The gospel must first be preached to all nations

All men will hate you because of me

There will be days of distress unequalled from the beginning

False Christs and false prophets will appear

There follows awesome apocalyptic scenes; the sun and moon darkened, the stars falling, and then

Men will see the Son of Man coming in clouds with great power and glory (verses 5-27).

Does this provide us with a vital clue to the central thrust of Jesus' ministry? Should we assume that today's church ought to emulate him? As the second millennium draws towards its close and millions of people tremble over social change, community collapse, moral chaos and dangerous international developments, should the church be sounding a more *apocalyptic* note? Many Christians believe so. This author's background was one of excited prophetic anticipation. 'Everything foretold in scripture before the Second Coming has now been fulfilled' we were earnestly assured. The next act in God's timetable is the Rapture, when God's people will be caught up in the clouds 'to be forever with the Lord', leaving the unbelieving world to suffer the horrors of tribulation and judgment. Several of my contemporaries (children of Christian homes) were converted through fear of discovering one day that their parents had disappeared leaving them alone to confront both the Antichrist and the False Prophet.

There were alternative versions, it has to be said. Israel's re-emergence as a nation was one 'fulfilled prophecy' but a still awaited sign was the rebuilding of the temple in Jerusalem. Worldwide church apostasy was another expected sign, half-unfolding already, although confusingly interrupted by reports in places of phenomenal missionary gains and of older Christian movements quickened by renewal. International Marxism was clearly the Antichrist, or at least his platform for world rule.

I recall with glee seeing more recently several cars in America whose rear-windows bore the slogan 'When the Rapture comes, this car will be without a driver'. Is this the way to understand the prophetic ministry of Jesus? Did he bequeath to his followers a prophetic timetable?

Without doubt he was seen by contemporaries as a prophet: 'Some say (you are) John the Baptist others say Elijah; and still others Jeremiah or one of the prophets' (Matthew 16:13-14). He spoke of himself as a 'greater than Jonah' (Matthew 12:38-41). Quite clearly he saw himself, and was seen by others, as a prophet in the great tradition of Israel.

But does that mean his task was to peer into the future and predict? Christians often believe so. The church apologetics of an earlier age has often argued something like this: 'The Old Testament prophets foretold the coming of Messiah and

Jesus offered himself as the fulfilment of those promises. In turn he pointed forward to further coming events, especially his own return in glory at the Second Advent. Thus the remarkable evidence of fulfilled prophecy bears witness both to the Bible's inspiration and to Christ's deity.' The argument goes like that.

There is much truth in this, but also some confusion. Jesus himself was both prophet and prophetic fulfilment. But prediction is not the principle ingredient of prophecy. The oracles of God are *not* to be regarded as a supreme example of supernatural forecasting; a kind of divine combination of Nostrodamus and Old Moore's Almanac. The Bible does *not* present veiled clues enabling us to construct a prophetic time-chart of a fixed immutable programme. It does *not* offer tantalizing glimpses of the-day-after-tomorrow's newspaper, with Jules Verne-like hints from Joel and Zechariah of the invention of the motorcar, the rise and fall of Stalin and the emergence of the European Common Market.

Israel's prophets (of whom Jesus was both supreme example and final fulfilment) rarely peered into the distant future. More often they addressed the immediate present, struggling to understand and thus convey to others what God was doing and saying in their immediate situation. It was not usually 'The Day of Judgment' or 'The End of the World' that occupied their thoughts, but rather the question 'What is happening in our society today?' A plague of locusts, an invitation to political alliance, a threat of invasion, a change of government, a social injustice—these were the events about which they 'prophesied'.[4]

---

4. Joel 1; Isaiah 18; Micah 1; Amos 5; Isaiah 6; Jeremiah 22.

Notice this. Most of the great prophets spoke and wrote during two particular periods. The eighth century BC saw Jerusalem threatened by Assyria, the city saved from disaster, but the northern Kingdom of Israel swept away. Two hundred years later the scenario was similar: Babylon threatened Jerusalem, took it by storm and destroyed the temple. In these events God's quarrel with his covenant people was displayed, said the prophets. And what was the subject of Jesus' great prophetic warning? The destruction of Jerusalem and the temple by Rome, consequent upon Israel's failure to recognize her day of opportunity and redemption.

Listen to Isaiah:

See now, the Lord, the LORD Almighty is about to take from Jerusalem both supply and support (Isaiah 3:1-3).

Listen to Jeremiah:

Flee for safety, people of Benjamin!
Flee from Jerusalem!
For disaster looms out of the north, even terrible destruction (Jeremiah 6:1-5).

Listen to Jesus:

Not one stone here will be left on another
Let those who are in Judea flee to the mountains
Jerusalem—your enemies will build an embankment against you (Mark 13:1-2, 14; Luke 19:41-44).

Three calls, in various combinations, were sounded by the prophets. There was *accusation*: God has a quarrel with his people. There was *judgment*: God will act against them. There was *appeal*: God urged his people to repent and come to a new mind. Precisely these features were prominent in Jesus' teaching, and not just in those parts popularly regarded as 'prophetic'. The call to repentance constantly sounded. God's quarrel with the religion of the leaders was repeatedly echoed. And the very phrase 'God's Kingdom is near' underlined the urgency of the appeal. 'Grasp what God offers and come under his gracious rule—or miss it and forever regret your loss': that was Jesus' message. The warning words on Olivet only reaffirmed the urgency in particularly stark form.

> O Jerusalem, Jerusalem, you who kill the prophets and stone those sent to you, how often I have longed to gather your children together—but you were not willing. Look, your house is left to you desolate (Matthew 23:37-38).

Matthew puts these remarks immediately before the further warning, 'not one stone will be left on another; every one will be thrown down' (24:2).

But is this to be understood as a warning and a plea, or as an invitation to peer forward through a prophetic timetable? The analogy of earlier prophets surely indicates the former. Prophecies were given, not to announce a fixed fate, but to avert a threatened disaster. Jonah (with whom Jesus specifically compared himself) warned of Nineveh's destruction within six weeks; it did not happen—precisely because the prophet was 'successful'.[5] The announcement of judgment was an implicit call to repentance. If people repented, the

---

5. Jonah 1:1-2 and 3:1-10. Note 'God did not bring the destruction he had threatened' (3:10).

judgment was averted. It happened in Isaiah's time in Jeru-salem, and the city was saved. Jeremiah, the weeping prophet, saw no subsequent repentance, and so the city fell. 'I longed to gather you—you would not' (said Jesus).

If the word 'success' is ever appropriate to a prophet, it must be applied not to one who succeeds in accurately spotting an unchangeable future, but to one who alters that future by his warnings and appeals. To coin a phrase, many prophecies were conditional, not immutable.

Promised Messiah

Of course one feature in Jesus' ministry set him apart from all other prophets. *He was in himself both prophecy and fulfilment.* He lived out, not so much a seer's timetable, as a constantly-repeated pattern and promise from God. He was himself the Son of Man from Daniel's vision, the Suffering Servant of Isaiah's song, the Anointed King of David's line (Daniel 7:13-14; Isaiah 53; Psalm 24).

Yet when he put forward those claims (as he repeatedly did in hint and allusion, in parable and in plain statement), it was not in terms of 'spot the prediction and look for the fulfilment'. When he chided people for failing to discern 'the signs of the times', it was not their slowness to guess the future but their inability to recognise the present that he reproved (Matthew 16:2-3). There was a pattern which they should have recognised. The Messianic 'promises' were usually presented as hints and pictures, foretastes and analogies; all from the experience of God's ancient people Israel.

This is why (for example) Matthew can 'see' Jesus in a promise of peace made to Micah, the exit of Israelites from Egypt, and the cry of widows heard by Jeremiah (Matthew 2:6

and 13-18 'fulfilling' Micah 5:2, Jeremiah 31:15 and Hosea 11:1).

Israel's Messiah reflected, repeated and fulfilled the pattern of Israel's experience of God. Jesus lived again the life of Israel. He fulfilled God's purpose for her which she failed to fulfil herself. He is *like* Israel coming out of Egypt, *like* Moses rescued from a child-murdering tyrant, *like* Jonah returning after three days to bring restoration to a penitent people, *like* Solomon amazing a pagan queen with his wise reign. He is *like* the prophet who suffers for his people's follies. He is even *like* the symbol of healing nailed to a pole in Israel's desert camp.

Apocalyptic seer?

Was Jesus an apocalyptist at all? Without doubt he was familiar with that dramatic form of social and religious protest, couched in cartoon-like melodramatic figures. It was a style peculiarly popular in his time, as it often is when social upheaval is at work. His own Bible contained several examples, especially in the books of Ezekiel, Daniel and Zechariah. He specifically quoted Daniel's visions, both in his Olivet warnings and at his trial before the high priest.[6]

The term *apocalypse* is taken from the Greek word for 'unveiling' or 'uncovering'. It is a kind of speech or writing that claims to reveal secrets, and is usually cast in the form of dreams, visions or messages from angels. It looks at the problem of evil (particularly institutionalised evil) and pictures war between the forces of good and bad, between God

---

6. Matthew 24:15 referring to Daniel 9:27; 11:31; 12:11. Matthew 26:62-64 referring to Daniel 7:13-14.

and Satan. It employs dramatic symbolism, and appeals to the emotions. It is always pessimistic about the immediate future but looks forward to the more distant future when God's kingdom will prevail and God's people will be vindicated. Within the Old Testament, the second half of Daniel is couched in these terms, and may have set a style that was imitated. The two centuries up to the appearance of Jesus produced many examples.[7] They were, so to speak, the popular religious paperbacks of the period. In the New Testament, the Book of Revelation provides a superb example, from whose opening words the genus gets its modern name.

But is that really the stuff of Jesus' Olivet warning? In fact there is little of the dark and lurid symbolism there. There is nothing symbolic about false religious teachers, war, famine, earthquake, religious persecution, moral apostasy and world-wide evangelism; this is all literal event. Jesus warned of it, and it all happened as he described it (Mark 13:1-23).

Only one paragraph really fits the style, as the sun is darkened, the stars fall, the sign of the Son of Man appears in the sky, and 'the angels gather his elect from the four winds' (verses 24-27). Interestingly, this is not Jesus' own choice of words, but is a mixture of quotations from the prophet Isaiah (13:10 and 34:4).

None of this gives any encouragement to prophetic time-charts and 'prophetic programmes'. Jesus himself disclaims any knowledge of 'the day or the hour' (verse 32). The purpose

---

7. Non-biblical examples of the apocalyptic style are the *Book of Enoch*; *Fourth Ezra*; the 'Dead Sea' document *War of the Sons of Light against the Sons of Darkness*. An early Christian example is *The Shepherd of Hermas*.

of the whole dramatic speech was to alert the readers' and hearers' spiritual awareness. 'Be on your guard' .... 'Keep watch' .... 'Do not let him find you sleeping' ... this is the note constantly sounded (verses 32-37).

Of course there is indeed an end-time emphasis, and the term *eschatology* would be more appropriate than *apocalyptic*. The disciples asked two questions that sparked off these words. 'When will these things happen?' and 'What will be the sign of your coming and of the end of the age?'[8] Most of Jesus' reply concerned the first; events already beginning to happen which inexorably led to the dreadful war and siege over thirty years later. The second question, that of his return in glory, remains still the Christian Hope. Watchfulness (as applied to both) does not mean preoccupation with the guessed-at future, but a present state of readiness and moral preparation. As Peter was later to put it, after a whole chapter devoted to the subject and couched in Olivet language, '... what kind of people ought you to be? You ought to live holy and godly lives as you look forward to the day of God and speed its coming' (2 Peter 3:11-12).

In the perceptive words of a modern writer, Mark chapter 13 is not like a road-sign that says 'End of Motorway 1 mile'. It is more like a line of hazard-lights, warning of dangers and changes ahead.[9] Jesus spoke of 'signs of the times', not to

8. Mark 13:1-4 cf. Matthew 24:1-3. Some Bible scholars suggest that Matthew, who mentions both questions and has extra material, has combined the answers given on two occasions. His addition of the three 'end-time parables' in his next chapter tends to suggest that.

9. Travis, *I Believe in the Second Coming of Jesus*, page 123. This whole book is a splendid example of a sane and biblical examination of the subject.

satisfy curiosity, nor to encourage speculation, but to strengthen faith and encourage commitment. Christians live in a world hostile to faith and goodness, heading for disaster, and desperately in need of their gospel. One day it will be 'too late'. We must get our priorities right.

Jesus and the future

If he did not provide clues to a futuristic crossword puzzle, did Jesus in any sense point to the future? He did indeed—by announcing that it had arrived! 'Tomorrow has come'— 'God's promised future is now bursting upon you'. That was the impact of his announcement that 'the kingdom of God is near' (Mark 1:14-15).

What psalmists had sung, prophets promised, kings groped after and visionaries glimpsed, was now happening *in the coming of Jesus*: 'Blessed are the eyes that see what you see. For I tell you that many prophets and kings wanted to see what you see, but did not see it' (Luke 10:23-24. cf. Luke 4:16-21 and John 5:24-27).

Modern scholars have called this first 'realised eschatology' and then, on reflection and more aptly, 'inaugurated eschatology'. The study of 'the Last Things' is no longer speculation or hope, but is becoming reality. The clock has started to tick; the End is beginning.

That was the message of the parables—almost every one of them. These are not simple tales with a moral twist, like Aesop's fables or the rabbis' stories. They are vivid announcements that the kingdom *has come* in Jesus, *is coming* through his gospel, and *will come* at his return.

The great campaign against sin, Satan and suffering has begun; the long awaited D-Day with God's Son as the liberating commander-in-chief. Parables of Rich Fool, Unprepared Bridesmaids, Great Supper and Good Samaritan are not cameos of teaching about farming, weddings, hospitality and social concerns. They are announcements that destiny is at the door, the Divine Bridegroom has come, the Messianic Banquet is ready, and racial barriers are banished in the New Community.[10]

What then of 'the shape of things to come'? It is indeed a general *shape* that the Christian is given. Disaster for the Jewish nation, capital and temple. An enlarged Israel, as Gentiles embrace the gospel. World evangelism, as the gospel is taken to every nation. Increasing chaos as natural and social structures buckle under the weight of mankind's wickedness and folly. Constant conflict between good and evil. And, one day, the personal return of Jesus in power and glory, when the 'now' and the 'not yet' of God's kingdom will come together.

This was no apocalyptic dreamer. This was God's Son, obedient to the heavenly vision; conscious of his calling to truth and suffering; preparing a people to follow him through both to a future so glorious that only the language of symbol can express. 'Prophecy' offers the Christian church today, not a maze of conundrums to thread, but a path of faith and servanthood to follow. And a message supremely appropriate for times of upheaval, change and fear.

---

10. Luke 12:13-21; Matthew 25:1-13; Luke 14:15-24; Luke 10:25-37.

Chapter 7

The Man who Chose Death

It is a strange fact, so familiar that we have forgotten how strange it is. The supreme Christian symbol is a cross. The most fiendishly cruel instrument of torture and execution ever devised by the twisted minds of vicious men is the sign of God's love. This extraordinary fact has come to be, because millions of Christians have seen in the progress of the man Jesus to his crucifixion the most exquisite expression of the love of God. God 'demonstrates his own love for us in this: While we were still sinners, Christ died for us' (Romans 5:8). Even the Romans who introduced crucifixion, probably as a development of Persian impalement, admitted its chilling, unbearable awfulness. Cicero called it 'the cruelest and most hideous of punishments—never may it come near the bodies of Roman citizens, never near their thoughts or eyes or ears.'[1] To Jews it carried the added horror of God's curse, as their Book of the Law so grimly said. No wonder the first Christian missionaries scandalized the religious world with their story of a crucified Messiah.[2]

An angry Jehovah's Witness once tackled me about it near the Garden Tomb in Jerusalem. 'Why do you church people insist on wearing a cross in your lapel or on a necklace?' (I

---

1. Stewart, page 179.
2. The scandal of the cross: Deuteronomy 21:23; Galatians 3:13; 5:11;
1 Corinthians 1:23.

wasn't doing either, but he rushed on.) 'If your grandmother had been tortured and shot by the Gestapo, would you pin a bullet to your lapel to celebrate?'

I replied, 'I might well, if she had offered herself to a firing-squad to enable me to escape and live. The instrument of her death would be the sign of her love and the symbol of my safety and gratitude.'

At the heart of the Jesus-story is his death. Every Gospel writer agrees on that, giving hugely disproportionate space to the week in which he died and the hours in which he hung on the cross. Scholars sometimes claim, with pardonable hyperbole, that the four Gospel records are passion narratives with lengthy introductions. What would one make, for example, of a biography of the late President John F Kennedy which devoted half its length to his entire life and the second half to the week that he died? Yet, to every Christian, there is no disproportion at all. Each learns to say with deep emotion, 'It was for me that Jesus died.'

How Christ saw it

What did Jesus say about his own death? First he spoke of *its inevitability*. The three Synoptic Gospel writers mark the crucial turning point in Jesus' ministry as that moment from which he began to speak of coming suffering and death. He had just drawn from Peter and his colleagues a clear confession: 'You are the Christ.' Then 'from that time on Jesus began to explain to his disciples that he must go to Jerusalem and suffer many things—that he must be killed and on the third day raised to life'.[3]

---

3. The turning-point: Matthew 16:13-28; Mark 8:27-33; Luke 9:18-27.

Mark and Luke both agree in spotlighting the same turning-point; the rest of their narratives (in Luke's case two-thirds of the whole) are built around the last journey to Jerusalem and to death. Matthew says the same with a different emphasis: from then onwards Jesus constantly returned to the theme of confrontation and suffering. John puts it differently again, by recording a succession of references to the vital 'hour' towards which the Saviour moves inexorably (John 2:4; 5:25-28; 7:30; 12:23-27; 16:32; 17:1).

All really say the same: he went deliberately to his death. He was not dragged to it, but walked towards it in the freedom of his own unconquered soul. 'The Son of Man [came] to give his life as a ransom'. 'I lay down my life. No one takes it from me, but I lay it down of my own accord' (Mark 10:45; John 10:17-18).

The reason why

The question of why he died can be explored in several directions. In the next chapter I want to follow some of the pressures and power struggles that drove events towards arrest, accusation, trial and sentence. But first we need to look at both the immediate circumstances and the comments that Jesus himself made upon them. Then we can examine his direct teaching about the meaning of that death which he faced with unswerving purpose.

The first can be related bluntly and briefly. In a short public ministry of perhaps three to four years, he outraged every prejudice, infuriated every pressure-group, insulted every vested interest and angered every sect and party in the turbulent provinces of Judaea and Galilee. But the chilling fact is that those who first hated him, then plotted against him and finally hounded him to death, were not outstandingly wicked people. They shared the vices and vanities common to us all.

Why should that lead to such murderous violence? We should not be puzzled. In today's society murder can be motivated by the colour of someone's skin, the shape of their religion, the name of his tribe, the attractiveness of her body, or even the fact that he tries to prevent a petty act of vandalism or crime. Barely-repressed violence is part of the human condition—expressed sometimes by the vicious act, more often by the violent word—as Jesus said (Matthew 5:21-26).

The first expressed wish to kill Jesus was caused by his healing of a sick man on the Sabbath day. This seems to have happened within weeks of the start of his ministry (Mark 3:1-6). Like this first incident, much of the opposition and hatred stirred up by Christ's ways and words was due to a fundamental clash between his values and theirs. His attitude to the marginalised, his definition of goodness, his balance of priorities, his emphasis on peace, forgiveness and reconciliation; all of these were offensive and infuriating.

But threatening, too. He threatened the cynical opportunism of the priestly establishment. He threatened the violent schemes of the Zealots. He threatened the meticulous definitions of the Pharisees. The threat was not physical, but moral and spiritual. They simply had to get rid of him.

A deeper purpose

Was Jesus' deliberate walk towards suffering simply the courageous act of a committed man who weighs the odds, counts the cost, and presses on? Much modern thinking, both 'popular' and 'scholarly' suggests so. The traditional view of a heaven-sent Redeemer moving towards Calvary with saving intent is dismissed. That, we are told, is read back into the story with early church hindsight. Good Jews that they were, once the first disciples recovered from the shock of the crucifixion, and developed an assurance that Jesus was some- how still close to them, they ransacked their Old Testament scriptures for hints, symbols and prophecies of a suffering Messiah—a totally new idea.

But no-one, we are assured, would have found such a sin- atoning Messiah in their Bibles had they not determined to put him there first. The Gospel writers, we are led to believe, behaved rather like a mining prospector who salts his patch with a few tiny gold nuggets in order to sell off his claim. This idea is trotted out so often that it begins to sound correct simply through its constant repetition.

In actual fact the record tells us something quite different. So does the ever increasing accumulation of evidence from first century Jewish thought. Ironically, this is being redis- covered by new Jewish believers in Jesus, even as their more liberal Gentile counterparts continue to deny it.

Jesus not only spoke of his coming death as inevitable. He hinted at its purpose as he walked towards it. He instituted a custom rich with meaning as he approached its shadow. And he expounded its fullest meaning when he came out of the shadows again into resurrection life and glory.

A pregnant passage in Mark, the earliest and shortest Gospel, gives three word-pictures drawn by Jesus himself, and set in the context of his determined journey to Jerusalem and suffering (Mark 10).

At the heart of the scene is an obtuse and embarrassing argument between members of his beyt as to who should have top jobs in the coming Kingdom. Jesus shames them out of their place-seeking, by speaking of three grim experiences which they would do well to consider. There is a cup that he must drink (verse 38); there is a baptism that he must endure (verse 38 again); there is a ransom that he must pay (verse 45).

All of them convey images of violence and of pain. The draining or drinking of a cup was a familiar Old Testament simile for the endurance of pain from God's hands. For example, 'In the hand of the Lord (is) a cup of foaming wine poured out on the wicked—drink it to the very dregs.' Moreover, drinking from a cup with someone else was a Jewish idiom for sharing their fate. The obvious meaning to their ears (though bewildering enough, to be sure) was that Jesus would somehow drink to the dregs other people's judgment, and share the deserved fate of others. Were they really so keen on that kind of top job?[4]

Secondly, he spoke of a baptism he had to endure. The literal meaning is immersion in, or total identification with, some life-threatening situation. Again there were Old Testament precedents like 'All your waves and breakers have swept over me'. The familiar Jewish custom of that time of plunging Gentile converts in a mikvah (ceremonial pool of water) also spoke of the old life abandoned—an image soon to be taken up by Christian Baptism.[5]

Finally, and most eloquently of all, Jesus invokes the image of ransom-payment. 'Even the Son of Man did not come to be served, but to serve, and to give his life as a ransom for many'. A ransom is a price paid for someone else's release

---

4. The Cup of Suffering: Psalm 75:8; Isaiah 51:17-23; Jeremiah 49:12; Lamentations 4:21; Ezekiel 23:31-34.

5. Immersion-baptism: Psalms 42:7; 69:2; Isaiah 43:2; Romans 6:1-7.

from bondage or captivity. Familiar in the culture of that day, especially in the slave-market, it has found terrifying new illustration in the late twentieth century with its hostage-taking. A ransom is a price paid for freedom. Redemption is the process of paying it.

In the immediate context of the story, the price paid will rescue the disciples from the selfish and destructive slavery of wanting to be master. At the heart of all truly Christian leadership is the example and motivation of the crucified and risen Lord who gave his life precisely to set us free to serve. This is a theme to which Mark constantly returns, in his vivid picture of the Servant King.

But again, there are strong Old Testament undercurrents in the words used. All Jewish history found its source and starting place in that great act of redemption called Passover, when blood was shed to set a whole people-group free from Egyptian slavery. Moreover the striking phrase 'for the many' echoed the often-pondered prophetic picture of Isaiah's suffering servant who 'justified the many' by 'bearing their iniquities', who 'bore the sin of many and made intercession for the transgressors'. (Isaiah 53:11-12, but see the whole chapter.) In turn, the apostle Paul will echo the words, so striking that they simply must have passed into the rote-catechizing of the early church and thus came to him: 'The man Christ Jesus who gave himself as a ransom for all men' (1 Timothy 2:5, 6).

The message is clear. Christ died to bear a punishment deserved by others, to share a suffering destined for others, and to pay a price that set others free.

A suffering Messiah?

Then what of the often-suggested objection that neither Jesus nor his Jewish followers could really have 'seen' something in the great hope and promise of the Messiah-King that simply wasn't there? Many modern Jewish people sincerely believe that to be so. Advertisements appear in today's *Jerusalem Post* newspaper, offering correspondence courses or cassettes warning the gullible not to be misled by absurd Christian misuse of the Messianic promises.

From their point of view, the irritation is understandable. One thoughtful Israeli told me quite bluntly, 'The two pictures are simply incompatible and contradictory at every point. The Messiah is a powerful figure of authority who brings recognizable peace and justice to this real world. Your Christ is a suffering figure of weakness who brings unquantifiable blessings to an invisible other-world. Trying to turn one into the other must rate as the biggest con-trick in religious history.'

But that is not so. Earnest Jewish students of their own scriptures before and after Jesus found *both* pictures of the Messiah. They were puzzled. They tried various ways to reconcile the two pictures. Some floated the idea of two, three or even four distinct Messiahs. But the promises and prophecies were certainly there for all to see. Modern Jewish believers in Jesus are rediscovering that fact.

One described his journey of discovery to me. 'As I studied Messianic promise, this thought came powerfully to me: what more could Messiah be than Jesus of Nazareth already is?'

Much Jewish thinking focused on the lovely 'Suffering Servant' pictures from Isaiah's great collection of prophetic songs. Here are a few comments from Jewish scholars which might well have been made by a convinced Christian (except of course that the Messiah is never called Jesus).

> The Messiah, the Son of David, as it is written 'a man of pains and known to sickness'.
>
> Messiah, bear the suffering and punishment of thy Lord, with which he chastises thee for the sins of Israel, as it is written, 'He is pressed for our rebellion and cursed for our iniquities'.
>
> Since the Messiah bears our iniquities — it follows that whoever will not admit (this) must endure and suffer them himself.[6]

A renowned Jewish scholar in Israel admitted to a colleague of mine, 'I am almost sure that Jesus of Nazareth was the Son of Man depicted in Daniel's vision, though I cannot use the Greek categories of the church creeds to describe him.' The vision he referred to is that quoted by Jesus in response to the challenge at his 'trial'—'Are you the Messiah?' Although pictured by Daniel as kingly and glorious, he stands identified with God's suffering people. This same book of prophecies led to a widespread belief amongst Jews in Jesus' day that martyrdom for the truth of God not only atoned for the martyr's own shortcomings but somehow offered expiation for the whole nation—the 'many' already referred to.[7]

---

6. Quotations are from the Midrash Thanhumi, the Midrash Cohen, and Rabbi Eliyyah de Vidas. Denton (ed) *Tishrei* magazine Volume 1 No 4, Summer 1993. This lists many other quotations stretched over fifteen centuries, in the article 'The Messiah' by Arnold G Fruchtenbaum.

7. The Son of Man: Daniel 7:13-14; Matthew 26:62-64. This, of course, was Jesus' own favourite description of himself, as his frequent use of it underlines. Notice how Daniel 12:1-3 also expresses the clearest hope of resurrection to be found in the Old Testament.

In other words there was nothing inconsistent or unlikely about Jesus himself drawing the message of his own Messianic suffering from his Jewish Bible. His apostles did not have to put it there, it was there already, awaiting fulfilment.

Truth for today

What then of the way we share the good news of a suffering Saviour? Good news it most certainly is; what better announcement could there be than that of a price already paid, a work already completed, a door already opened, and a pardon available to all who ask?

Unfortunately, it is open to mis-statement and misunderstanding. Modern Christian communicators have given way to the lure of cheap grace rather then free grace. There is no shortage of pulpit-stars or television pulpiteers ready to assure us that because Christ suffered for us, we are invited to a pain-free, problem-free, pressure-free life. The Christian's birthright (we are told) is instant rescue from everything that hurts, and instant gratification of every good desire— even of somewhat dubious desires.

It may be offered with sincerity and sprinkled with biblical verses out of context, but it is a gross travesty of the message of the cross.

A fellow evangelist of mine bears the scars of a sacrificial ministry that has inspired hundreds worldwide to costly discipleship and mission. In 1994 he addressed an Asian conference attended by several hundred. In the same city, ten times as many gathered to hear another preacher whose slogan was, 'Health, wealth and happiness can be yours through the cross of Christ'. More attractive—but is it true? The senior schoolgirl mocked for remaining a virgin; the doctor refused promotion because of his conscience; the local government official sacked for declining to lie; the businessman in financial trouble because he honestly declares his profits; the aid-worker who contracts a disease through her work; the parents hated as cranks because they protest against immorality taught in school—all of these Christians carry a cross.

The true evangelist certainly offers the 'glorious exchange' (as the Puritans called it) whereby we are given his goodness because he carried our badness.[8] But to turn that exchange into one in which the Son of God allegedly removes all our problems, pains, pressures and perils is simply to pave a path to disillusionment. It was never promised this side of heaven. It is not the message of the One who bore his cross and invited us to carry ours.

It is fascinating (and sobering) to see how almost every reference to the cross on the lips of Jesus is accompanied by an invitation to die with him as well as to live through him. The reader can easily check it out for himself.[9] The same emphasis is seen in the apostolic writings. The only way to avoid the pain is to cut the promises in half and ignore fifty percent. And a half-gospel is not a gospel at all.

---

8. The glorious exchange: 2 Corinthians 5:20-21.
9. Christ's death for us and ours with him: Matthew 16:21-28; Mark 10:35-45; John 12:20-33; Galatians 2:20; 6:14; 1 Peter 2:20-25; 1 John 1:5-7.

Chapter 8

The Man who Exposed the Powers

To my mind, one of the most haunting and atmospheric places in old Jerusalem is the area that still encloses some of the remains of the Antonia Fortress. For that grim citadel, towering over the Temple area, witnessed two of those several mock-trials that presaged the death of Jesus. [1]

It was a large area, and its vestiges are liable to crop up in unexpected places. The Roman road, ribbed to assist chariot wheels, can be spotted in the floor of a church and a convent. A Palestinian primary school and a religious gift-shop have parts of the south-east tower incorporated into their building. A piece of the Ecce Homo arch, where Pilate announced enigmatically 'Behold the man' is behind the altar of a Roman Catholic church. Another part protrudes over today's narrow shopping street as it slopes down from the Bethesda Pools area where Jesus healed a lame man on the Sabbath. The famous and oft-visited 'King's game' (a kind of simplified chess, with living prisoners used as pawns and pieces) lies below a

---

1. Several studies of Christ's 'trials' have attempted to analyse the motives, the laws applied (and misapplied) and the exact order of events. Many of them are weakened by the authors' disinclination to accept the Gospel accounts as wholly truthful. To my mind the best and most readable is still Morison's book *Who Moved The Stone?*

convent where gentle-faced nuns pray for the conversion of visiting tourists—and then recommend a visit to the Garden Tomb where they will hear the gospel again. This could well be the place where the King of Sorrows was mockingly crowned with twisted thorn-twigs, 'the crown of pain to three and thirty years'.

Appropriately enough, the venues for the other trials are now Christian buildings. The citadel where Jesus briefly stood before Herod Antipas, the palace of Caiaphas where he was examined as to his claims to Messiah's crown—even the 'Gethsemane' (olive-press cave) where he was first arrested—all are places where now you will hear the story of redeeming love sung, prayed, preached and read. I have seen people turning to Jesus in them all. One thing is painfully clear: the man who had defied the 'powers' that dominated ancient Palestine (religious, political and social) found them united in their detestation of him and their determination to destroy him. Yet we find repeatedly that they are truly on trial, not he.

Passover focus

The annual feast of Passover (attendance at which was practically obligatory for every adult Jew) became the focus of those powers, since each needed to be represented in the holy city at that particular time. All had their own reasons for wanting the radical rabbi crushed. All revealed themselves in their worst and truest colours. And, in several remarkable statements, the New Testament tells us that the Son of God exposed and defeated them all, through his exposure to them and apparent destruction by them. What defeated them was his steadfast refusal to submit to their pressure, retreat before their power, or accept their embrace. He exhausted their venom, and demonstrated the superior power of self-giving love that is the heart of God.

The struggle for power

Motivating every group that accused, condemned and crucified Christ, was some definition of *power*. The Sadducean priestly hierarchy represented *religious power*. To preserve it, the temple authorities walked a tightrope of political appeasement. On the one hand they accepted Rome's authority, most pointedly symbolized by the huge Antonia fortress which actually occupied one corner of the temple complex itself, its watchful guards ready to advance at the double to quell any disturbance in the sacred portals.[2] The Gospel writers and Josephus both picture that scenario. On the other hand, they met religious aspirations of the populace with their highly sophisticated and profitable organization of temple services and sacrifices. Immense numbers of residents and pilgrims constantly flowed in and out of the temple courts. This in turn shaped the whole economy of the city-state. Not for nothing was the temple cynically described as the bazaar of Annas.[3]

Traditional Power

If the Sadducees symbolized economic and religious power, then the *Pharisees* personified *the power of tradition*. Their 'politics of holiness' was an attempt to define the people of God in terms of visible separation. Their rules of *kosher* food

2. Roman intervention in the Temple, Luke 13:1; Acts 21:27-36. Also numerous references in Josephus: *Antiquities* and *War of the Jews*.

3. Contemporary criticism of the Temple.

made every housewife's kitchen a shrine, every family meal a sacrament. Their 'fencing' of the Law (for example at least two hundred Sabbath sub-regulations) reduced external conformity to a fine art. The intention was good, the original impetus biblical, but the eventual outcome was pernicious. A few religious lay-teachers, armed with the immense weight of tradition and precedent, defined exactly who was inside and who was outside the charmed circle of the People of God. The power to excommunicate is power indeed—and wide open to corruption and exploitation. Jewish and Christian history have both provided melancholic demonstration of that.[4]

Armed Power

The third power base in Jerusalem was that of Rome, already referred to. Its soldiers were omnipresent, its tax-collectors omnivorous, its physical power stunning. Naked force and cold fear were its weapons. The reason why the frequent crucifixions always took place beside major highways was to strike constant, subduing terror into every passer-by. In exchange, the subjugated people were given the Pax Romana, an enforced but impressive administrative system and an ordered existence—with generous opportunities to become Roman citizens.

In Jesus' time, Rome was represented by Governor Pilate. One contemporary described him as inflexible, merciless and obstinate.[5] Both Josephus and the New Testament refer to

---

4. Excommunication: see John 9:22.
5. A description of Pilate quoted by Philo, a Jewish philosopher in Egypt roughly contemporary with Jesus. He quotes a letter from King Agrippa to the Emperor Caligula (Philo: Ad Gaium 38, page 65). See Stott, page 50.

several different quarrels between Pilate and the Jewish authorities, in which he swung between cruel stubbornness and weak wavering. Each time he had to give way. His reports to Rome must have made interesting reading.[6]

Kept in place by the real power of Rome was the puppet-power of *local administration*, as represented by the family successors of Herod the Great. That half-Jewish usurper had grasped local authority by force, consolidated it by marriage to a Jewish princess, fortified it with brilliant building projects, and preserved it by unspeakable cruelties. He held a kind of fiefdom under Rome, and played religious power with one hand and political power with the other, rebuilding the temple for the religious, and establishing several beautiful pagan cities for the irreligious.[7] We might fairly describe Herodian power, in its various manifestations as *manipulative power* or (dare we say it?) *entrepreneurial power*.

Herod's life ended miserably in BC 4 (which helps us to pin down the date of Jesus' birth, since the tyrant was still murderously alive up to two years after Christ's birth). His puppet-kingdom was divided between his sons, most of them as revoltingly self-seeking and corrupt as himself. Herod Antipas was allocated Galilee and Peraea, and he it was who had John the Baptist beheaded after a drunken party. Other-

---

6. Pilate's quarrels with Jewish authorities: Josephus, *War*, 2:9: 169 and 175. One concerned the smuggling of 'idolatrous' Roman standards into the temple area. The other involved the seizure of temple funds to finance a new aqueduct. Both provoked riots that forced Pilate to withdraw.

7. Herod the Great's building schemes. These included the rebuilding of the Temple in Jerusalem and the 'new' pagan city of Caesarea-by-the-sea.

wise known as Herod the Tetrarch because he ruled only a quarter of the Jewish territory, he was once referred to by Jesus as 'that fox'. It was he who briefly interviewed Jesus during the hours before the crucifixion—a scene in which, to quote Alexander Whyte, he revealed the incurable shallowness of his character, and behaved more like a circus ringmaster than a magistrate.[8]

The final figure in the equation might be labelled *popular power*. The Zealot movements, religious, patriotic and populist, were committed to passive resistance at least, and urban guerilla warfare at most. Their popular uprisings usually convulsed Galilee, but one had obviously taken place in Jerusalem itself, shortly before Jesus' own arrest. Barabbas, whose cross Jesus literally bore, was one of their leaders, and the two 'robbers' whose crosses flanked his were really insurrectionists as one of the biblical writers makes clear.[9]

It is hardly necessary to point out the twentieth century equivalent of that first century 'tendency'; those patriotic fronts and freedom fighters who begin with a just cause and sink to levels of terror and oppression as deep and dark as those they seek to overthrow. Nor need we look far in politics, commerce and organised religion, to see modern equivalents of those other powers that manoeuvred for advantage around the arrested prisoner called Jesus of Nazareth.

Here then was that parallelogram of competing forces which surrounded the lonely figure at his trials and sufferings. Each is conveniently symbolized by a named figure. *Caiaphas*

---

8. Herod Antipas. Mark 6:14-28; Luke 13:31f.; 23:7ff.

9. Zealots at the cross: Matthew 27:11-26; 27:38; Mark 15:6-15; Luke 23:39-43.

stood for religious power and for 'the Establishment'. *Pilate* symbolized political and military power. *Herod Antipas* manipulated entrepreneurial power—and fixed a deal with Pilate in the very process that pointed Jesus to his death. It is a point often made by preachers that the shallow fickleness of popular opinion is displayed in the swift change from 'Welcome to the Son of David' on Palm Sunday, to 'Away with him—crucify him' on Good Friday morning. A close examination of both events makes it very unlikely that they were identical crowds. The mob on Friday morning had Jesus 'sprung on them' as they arrived to demand Barabbas' release. Nevertheless it is a point well made; nothing is more exploitable than 'public opinion'.

Only the Pharisaical Party fail to come up with a really determined spokesman, although they were certainly involved in the conspiracy. Instead, two men actually attempt to make some kind of defence of the prisoner: Nicodemus and Joseph of Arimathaea. This is one of several hints that the Pharisee Party was not wholly opposed to Jesus. As undoubtedly the most 'spiritual' Jewish movement, it found itself pulled two ways by the strange rabbi who could with one hand point to the holiness of God's commands and with the other beckon to outcasts who outraged every respectable principle of behaviour. So there was protest in this camp—but the dead weight of tradition and the frightening power of religious anger prevailed.

So the grim power-struggle goes on. Caiaphas and his colleagues bend every rule and gamble on the dangers of precipitating a riot against the value of silencing this radical.

They cynically agree that one man's death could profit the whole nation—especially their grip on it. Pilate, trapped by

his own bungling and controversial record, backs off from yet
another confrontation that could lose him his job. Herod
Antipas neatly passes the buck back to Pilate, but first derives
a bit of bored amusement from the situation (Dorothy Sayers
imagines him asking afterwards with a yawn why nothing
interesting or important ever seems to happen).[10]

The various charges levelled against the prisoner reflect
echoes of the real power struggle that was going on, even
though some were absurd and nonsensical.[11] This man threatened the temple. He made Messianic claims. He called
himself Son of God. He stirred up the nation and spoke against
the tax system. He declined to perform miracles-to-order for
the local authority. He claimed to be king, but was equivocal
about the nature of his authority. A vote for him was a vote
against Caesar. These were the charges levelled against him,
all speaking more significantly of those who levelled the
accusations than of him who bore them. The scenes shine a
ghastly light on that manipulation of power which is a feature
of fallen people and a fallen society.

We can list examples known to us. If we consider abstrac-
tions, then we can talk of domestic tyranny, school bullying,
political lobbying, peer pressure, cultural momentum, military threat or faceless market forces. But each has its personal
example; men and women not unlike you and me. The
bullying husband and manipulative mother-in-law; the school
thug and the headmaster who won't deal with him because he
has his own career to watch; the smooth-talking local coun-

10. In her 1940 playcycle *The Man Born to be King*.

11. The charges against Jesus: Matthew 26:59-65; Luke 22:70-71;
23:1-25; John 18:28-37.

cillor and the power-hungry politician whose voices sound strangely different for a few weeks before an election, but then revert to type: these are all familiar. So, in religious circles, is the church leader whose 'gift of administration' cloaks a need to dominate others. So is the trouble-fomenter at deacon's court or church meeting (he or she may be in favour of renewal *or* tradition) who hides personal insecurity under a deep desire to manipulate.

In Dorothy Sayers' instructions to actors in the trial scene of *The Man Born to be King*, she suggests that the mob-extras imagine a parochial church council in one of its crucifying moods.

> Oh break, oh break, hard heart of mine!
> Thy weak self-love and guilty pride
> His Pilate and his Judas were;
> Jesus, our Lord, is crucified!

But the silent prisoner did more than expose and shame this pride and power. He conquered it, as he said he would.

> Having disarmed the powers and authorities, he made a public spectacle of them, triumphing over them by the cross (Colossians 2:15).

How did he conquer? By refusing to be seduced or corrupted by that power. He rejected the options offered to him. That rejection was seen earlier, in his temptation in the wilderness, in his Sermon on the Mount, in the prayer he taught his disciples, in the way he handled miraculous power and in the way he chose to ride into Jerusalem on Palm Sunday.

Hours before his 'trials' he fought and won the battle afresh in Gethsemane.[12]

Undeflected by the pleas of friends, the offers of allies, the threats of enemies and the whispers of Satan, he went on his way to accusation, suffering and death, in total obedience to his divine mission and mandate.

By seemingly surrendering to the pull and pressure of the power-structures and their human representatives, he threw them off balance. Silent in the face of accusation, he allowed his accusers to have their way, breaking silence only twice to offer them saving truth ('Those who love truth recognize me', and, 'I am the Christ and you shall see ...'.) and once to pray for their forgiveness ('they know not what they do').

Pardon the mundane analogy: We see the power manipulators falling over backwards like a tug-of-war team who heave on the rope only to find there is no resistance.

By surrendering to them, he refused to be enslaved by them, and thus defeated them. He 'disarmed them' (as we have heard Paul say) by silencing their persuasive lies and thus exposing them.

No wonder Jesus was so direct and uncompromising with everyone, especially his closest friends who tried to divert him from the cross. Only by holding firm to the way of the cross could he finally destroy all the spiritual powers which hold men and women in bondage, and

---

12. See Prior pages 32-53 and 124-157. I am hugely indebted to David Prior for this searching exposition of what Jesus meant by power. It should be compulsory reading for all religious leaders—and not least for those who seek to be evangelistic media-manipulators!

which concentrate their impact on individuals (such as Herod, Caiaphas and Pilate) and institutions (such as the Sanhedrin) with the greatest worldly power.[13]

Walking and speaking the way of the cross

The question comes back once more. Does our message of the cross bear any resemblance to Christ's path towards it and bearing of it? One of the starkest tragedies of Christian history is the church's failure to embrace the cruciform victory over the corrosive influence of power play.

Some examples are obvious (and comfortably remote from the average Evangelical). See how the very shape of the cross is a fear and offence to Jews and Muslims because it was worn on the shields and banners of murderous 'crusaders'. South American Indians have painful race-memories too: the crucifix was carried ahead of soldiers, traders and missionaries as a symbol of military might, economic power and religious violence. This is all sufficiently far away to comfortably condemn.

But what of ecclesiastical power struggles, whether at the level of Anglican national synod or local Brethren eldership? What of the elderly church-trustee who boasts 'this church has had three tries at spiritual renewal and I've seen off all three of them' (a remark I report ten days after hearing it)? What of the blatant manipulativeness of mass-evangelists who pull out every stop on the organ of emotional appeal, prosperity dreams and cultural conformity? What of the coercion and subliminal suggestiveness of the power-hungry group leader whose language may sound biblical but whose

13. Prior, pages 156-157

motive is the opposite of that one who 'came not to be served but to serve'?

That last quotation brings us back full-circle to the great ransom passage preserved by Mark. I was taught when preparing for ordination that it is the bottom line for understanding Christian 'ministry'. Yet the very word *minister* has so often been turned upside down into the image of the clergyman as the man in charge, the man with power, the man to obey. Of course the word really means simply 'servant'. Here are the words of Mark 10:42-45:

> Jesus called them together and said, 'You know that those who are regarded as rulers of the Gentiles lord it over them, and their high officials exercise authority over them. *Not so with you.* Instead, whoever wants to become great among you must be your servant, and whoever wants to be first must be slave of all. For even the Son of Man did not come to be served, but to serve, and to give his life as a ransom for many.'

Victories of the cross are only won in this spirit.

Chapter 9

The Man who Conquered Satan

The New Testament insists that Jesus, by dying, defeated evil. The writers certainly see it that way. The reason the Son of God appeared was to destroy the devil's work (1 John 3:8). He suffered death so that he might destroy him who holds the power of death—that is the devil (Hebrews 2:14). In picturesque symbolic language, the Bible's last book describes victory over the dragon 'through the blood of the Lamb' (Revelation 12:1-12).

It was a truth eagerly seized upon by spokesmen for the worldwide church, as the Faith broke out of its Jewish culture. The Greek, Roman and Oriental worlds were grimly aware of the powers of darkness, disorder, fear, obsession and evil. For Christians, there was added the persecution of paganism. Elaborating on biblical symbolism they bore witness to the cross as a weapon of destruction forged against the powers of darkness. Some even spoke rather oddly of the offered life of Christ as a bait which lured the devil into swallowing the hook which 'landed' him and destroyed him.

A thousand years later, Martin Luther proclaimed *Christus Victor*, the Christ who conquers through death. John Stott says, 'Luther's hymns and catechisms reverberate with joy that God has rescued us from the monster or tyrant—who previously held us in the captivity of sin, law, curse and death.'[1] Two centuries after Luther, the Wesley brothers preached and sang in England of the cross that 'puts all our foes to flight' and the Name at which 'devils fear and fly'.

Is this a case of slightly feverish imagination and aggressive religious symbolism? No, for Jesus himself encouraged such attitudes in his life and words as he moved towards the cross.

He spoke often of the sinister reality of Satan. Usually in metaphorical language (how else?) he likened the enemy to the despotic master of a household, the ruler of a malign kingdom, a god claiming worship, a strong but defeated soldier, and 'the prince of this world'.[2]

He declared his own life, teaching, miracles and suffering as a prelude to Satan's downfall. The casting out of demons in particular and the delivering of people from sickness and estrangement in general, were shown as declaration of war on Satan's kingdom and demonstrations of God's Kingdom.[3]

He delegated authority to his disciples: the seventy-two as well as the twelve.[4] In one dramatic scene when they returned flushed with success from a kingdom-mission of preaching, healing and exorcism, he exclaimed, 'I saw Satan fall like lightning *from* heaven', but immediately added that more significant was the simple knowledge that their names were written *in* heaven (Luke 10:17-24).

---

1. Stott, page 229.
2. Jesus' word-pictures of Satan: Matthew 10:25; 12:26; Luke 4:5-7; Mark 3:27; John 12:31.
3. God's rule and the expulsion of demons: Luke 11:20-22.
4. Christ gives authority to his disciples: Matthew 10:7-8; Mark 6:7; Luke 10:9.

In other words, conversion and acceptance in God's family is the fundamental miracle, and the surest sign that God's Kingdom has come. In the splendid words of one theologian, commenting on this passage:

> Jesus' visionary cry of joy leaps over the interval of time—and sees in the exorcisms performed by the disciples the dawn of the annihilation of Satan. This stage had already been reached: the evil spirits are powerless, Satan is being destroyed, paradise is opened, the names of the redeemed stand in the book of life.[5]

Modern commentators often claim (rather condescendingly) that obsession with demons was common in Jesus' world. The suggestion is that he employed the accepted mythological language in order to declare all the more vividly that people can be set free from whatever social, psychological, physical or spiritual bondages grip them. But the safest assumption is that he who was truth personified chose to speak in the most accurate, helpful, truthful and liberating way.

In fact his words and deeds bear little resemblance to those of 'his time'. They were totally unprecedented. The announcement of 'Satan vanquished now' simply cannot be paralleled in the ceremonies of the priests, the teaching of the rabbis, the deeds of the charismatic hassidim, or the meditations of the Qumran Essenes. In this, as in all else, Jesus stands alone.

Satan cast out
The apostle John records a remarkable scene during the week that would end in the crucifixion (John 12:20-33). Some

---

5. Joachim Jeremias, page 95.

Grecianised Jews on pilgrimage to the holy city asked to interview Jesus. The disciples no doubt saw this as an invitation to a whole new world of opportunity. Perhaps they could use it to prise the Master away from the dangers of a city which his warnings and their own fears filled with chill foreboding of rejection and suffering. If Jerusalem disowned him, the great wide world of the Diaspora (the Jewish Dispersion) might open to him. A new harvest-field, full of possibilities! Jesus' response pulls the shadows around them again. There can be no harvest until seed has fallen into the ground and died.

But the very mention of dying seed and living harvest recalls Satan's whisper that has never been long silent—'Why go the way of suffering when there are other ways to win mankind's loyalty?' [6] Jesus is 'deeply troubled' (as soon he will be again in Gethsemane). Should he pray for some way to be 'saved from this hour?' No (he pulls himself together). 'No, it was for this very reason I came to this hour.' Rather, he will pray for God to be glorified.

What happens then? The battle joined and won once more; the tempting path that avoids the cross dismissed once more; the satanic whisper silenced once more; Jesus sees the devil's final defeat as certain. 'Now is the time for judgment on this world; now the prince of this world will be driven out.'

But what is the connecting link between Christ dying and Satan driven out? It is this—'When I am lifted up from the earth I will draw all men to myself' (John carefully adds 'He said this to show the kind of death he was going to die').

There it is. Christ's death undermined Satan's purpose of

---

6. The basic thrust of the temptations in the wilderness, and of Peter's rash protest at Caesarea Philippi (Matthew 4:1-11 and 16:21-23).

keeping people from God.[7] His cross exposed the devil's lies, silenced his false whispers about God, crippled his ability to deceive and damn, silenced his accusations, and loosed his grip. In the fine words of another modern scholar:

> He drew on himself the despotic fury which was crushing the world, and by dying to it without submitting to it, he defeated it. He remained obedient to the end because his love went right to the end. That is why St Paul concludes triumphantly: He stripped the rulers.[8]

The long conflict

Grasp this, and we see the Gospel accounts of Christ's life (as well as his death) in a new light. They begin, as we have seen, with the story of his 'temptation in the wilderness'.[9] There he decisively rejected the subtle suggestions of other ways to achieve domination over people—alternatives to God's call to submission, service and suffering. The temptation returned, of course, and he recognized its source even when his friend and disciple Peter was its well-meaning mouthpiece: 'Get behind me, Satan' (Matthew 16:21-23).

That too explains why the desert victory led immediately to the powerful Galilee ministry. Evil spirits fled, physically bound people were liberated, good news was spread, the kingdom was declared.

---

7. Satan keeps people from God: Genesis 3:1-5; 2 Corinthians 4:4; Revelation 12:9-12.
8. Wright, page 24.
9. Temptation in the wilderness: Matthew 4:1-11; Mark 1:12-13; Luke 4:1-13. Satan's 'claims' are seen in Luke 4:5-7; 2 Corinthians 4:4; Revelation 12:9.

And so the path led to those trial scenes already considered. There we see at work not only personal sin and corporate evil, but satanic opposition: 'The prince of this world is coming. He has no hold on me' (John 14:30); 'In regard to judgment, because the prince of this world now stands condemned' (John 16:11).

Corporate evil - but whose?

The subject of what Paul calls 'the powers' exercises the mind of many Christians today. [10] Does Satan infiltrate and exploit the social structures, human traditions and political drives that move governments, nations and peoples? Notice how the search for personal sexual freedom leads to permissiveness, obsession, perversion, and the undermining of family. See how a cry for social justice develops into the chant of merciless, murderous Communism. Shrink at the sight of pride in country or culture producing the monsters of massacre and ethnic cleansing. Notice how enterprise and market thinking release energies of exploitative greed and cynical injustice. See how religious zeal can grow into a monster of tyranny and cruelty.

Does all of this provide some clue to what Paul may mean by 'principalities, powers, and rulers of this world'? Is this another way of describing 'the prince of this world' who can apparently make realistic offers of the 'kingdoms of this world' to those who take his path? And if so, have we a clue here to the way in which, by shaming and exposing the corporate evils represented at his arrest, trial and execution,

---

10. For 'the powers' see Stott pages 233-5. A slightly different but complementary view is proposed in Berkhof, *Christ and the Powers*.

Jesus was also crippling the dark spirit-powers at work behind the scenes? (Colossians 2:15. cf. John 12:20-33 and Matthew 4:8-9).

How did Christ destroy the powers at his cross? In the fine words of Tom Wright again:

> He beat them at their own game. He drew onto himself the despotic fury which was crushing the world, and by dying to it without submitting to it, he defeated it.[11]

Death, where is thy sting?

But there is more. The Hebrew letter already quoted pictures Satan as enslaving people through the fear of death. So he does, as any observer of primitive animistic societies can readily see. But then he does it, too, in modern secular societies, where death is the one, unmentionable obscenity, never to be spoken of or faced. Satan enslaves those who 'all their lives were held in slavery by their fear of death' (Hebrews 2:14ff). He is the accuser (the very name Satan means literally that). Through tormented conscience and superstitious fear, he robs people of the realization that dying can be a simple step into the presence of God. An appointment with a welcoming Father becomes a dread meeting with a frowning Judge: that is Satan's success.

But by paying our penalty and bearing our curse, Christ has reversed the whole process again.

> The price is paid; see Satan flee away -
> for Jesus, crucified, destroys his power.

---

11. Wright, page 24. See his whole chapter entitled 'What I have written, I have written'.

No more to pay! let accusation cease;
In Christ there is no condemnation now!

Declaring liberty to captives

Again we are led to pose the question—How clearly are these truths expressed in our evangelism and church life today? For some, the answer to that challenge is found in a strong emphasis on 'signs and wonders' in general, and the casting out of demons in particular. The Lausanne Committee on World Evangelization (hardly a collection of charismatic fanatics) affirms:

> Signs should validate our evangelism. - We believe that (there) are evil personal intelligences under the command of the Devil. Demon possession is a real and terrible condition. Deliverance is possible only in a power-encounter in which the name of Jesus is invoked and prevails.[12]

Yet a word of caution is necessary too. C S Lewis warned that Satan greets with equal delight the materialist and the magician. He is equally able to manipulate the atheist who does not believe in his existence and the religious fanatic who thinks of little else.

Demons are not the cause of every ill from physical sickness to mental disturbance, from immoral behaviour to corporate evil. Exorcism is *not* the automatic answer to every problem the Christian confronts in himself or others. The current obsession with demonology amongst some evangeli-

12. Evangelicals and Social Concern—An Evangelical Commitment, No 21. (Grand Rapids Report 1982) pages 9-11 and 30-32.

cals and charismatics has more to do with a return to medieval superstition and fanaticism than with anything taught in the New Testament. Of course demons are a grim reality, and of course Christ's follower can confront them with quiet confidence in the power of the name of Jesus. But that is not an open invitation to the kind of bizarre demon hunting that is bringing dishonour to the Christian witness.[13]

Nevertheless, it remains a grim fact that the arch-enemy of mankind and of God is powerfully at work in today's collapsing society. Strange echoes of old forgotten superstitions are heard again. Witchcraft is quite widely practised. A 'New Age' tendency (hardly an organized movement) combines pseudo-scientific jargon with ancient occult practises. Mind-bending cults rise and flourish.

There are widespread examples, too, of emotional, psychic, physical or spiritual slavery. Alcoholism, drug abuse, solvent abuse, the obsessive pursuit of ever more colourful and bizarre sex, the careful and subtle promotion of what every civilized society and every major religion has regarded as perversion; the list seems endless. All of these can be seen as 'works of the Devil' without classifying them all sweepingly as 'Demon-possession'. All of them serve the double purpose of undermining people's humanity and alienating them from God. And to all of them the good news of a crucified but conquering Saviour needs to be addressed.

Sometimes that will lead to dramatic confrontation of the type portrayed not only in the life of Jesus but in the story of the apostolic church and in church history ever since.[14]

---

13. See my lengthy discussion and suggestions in Bridge, *Power Evangelism and the Word of God* pages 181-198.
14. Michael Green shows this conclusively, pages 226-233.

But melodrama is not the essential ingredient, and demons are not the invariable enemies.

God's Word systematically taught can be as powerfully effective as words of power dramatically spoken—and the former will be appropriate far more often than the latter.

The quiet influence of those who follow Christ in lowly self-giving (whether by indirect example or direct caring and counselling) is achieving every bit as much as the loudly trumpeted deliverance roadshows (in my own observation, a great deal more).

Prayer marches most certainly have their place and I believe can be argued biblically from Old and New Testament—but equally effective is the consistent intercessory prayer life of families and individuals, churches and communities who are committed daily to walking with God in the steps of Jesus.

Corporate evil certainly needs to be confronted with prayer and fasting that enters into the victory of the Christ who shamed it by suffering at its hands; who can doubt that this was a major ingredient in the collapse of Marxist Eastern Europe? But it also needs to be undermined by Christ's servants moving at every level in the 'corridors of power' and displaying attitudes to wealth, influence, manipulation, politics and persuasion, that demonstrate first their own liberation from 'the powers'.[15]

Most of all, the majestic simplicity of the gospel needs to be presented at every opportunity and by every method consistent with its principles and Lord. He conquered death by dying. He harrowed hell by descending to its depths. He lifted the curse by bearing it himself.

---

15. See Berkhof, chapters 5 & 6.

Chapter 10

The Man who Defeated Death

Almost every modern reconstruction of the 'life of Christ' finishes at the crucifixion. Some venture a closing chapter on the abiding influence of Jesus through the centuries. Others picture the stricken disciples gradually recovering from the shock and coming to the conclusion that somehow he is still with them. We are given touching pictures of early church leaders 'writing back' into the story little cameos featuring an empty tomb, angelic messages and meetings with Jesus—all to give expression to their growing conviction that somehow sin and death had not won.

Those that stop more abruptly at the cross suggest that this is where historical 'fact' ends in any measurable and meaningful sense, and the rest is in a different realm of faith, theology, speculation and mystical experience. Verifiable facts finish with the burial; interpretation may continue at leisure, according to inclination. So we are told.

But is this really so? In the Bible, the resurrection is not just something subjective that happened to the disciples. It is something objective that happened to Jesus. It is described in the same terms as his birth in Bethlehem, his childhood in Nazareth, his miracles in Galilee, his teaching in Jerusalem, and his death at Golgotha.

The New Testament authors write with a ring of truth.

Tested by any normal criteria, they are found to be truthful, accurate, consistent and convincing.

Visual aids

I spent fourteen months as chaplain of Jerusalem's 'Garden Tomb'. One task was to present the evidences for the Easter story. There was no requirement to 'prove' that it happened in that very spot; such certainty is neither desirable nor possible. What I had was a magnificent life-size visual aid. There was a first-century execution site beside a Roman road, outside the city wall. The hill bears some resemblance to a skull. Beside it is an ancient garden, as evidenced by water cisterns and winepress. In the garden is a tomb of the type described in the Gospel records. You can stoop, as John stooped, to peer through the low doorway. The burial chamber is on the right, as was the place where Jesus' body lay. The groove for the rolling-stone door enables you to calculate its considerable weight.[1] There are impressive coincidences, but not enough to say 'this is the place'—especially as there are other possible sites.[2]

---

1. *Details of the Garden Tomb* coinciding with biblical references: Skull-hill (Matthew 27:33; Luke 23:33), Garden nearby (John 19:41), Sepulchre-type tomb (Matthew 27:59-60), Low doorway (John 20:3-5), Body lying to the right of the door (Mark 16:5).

2. *Other possible sites:* The Church of the Holy Sepulchre has weighty historical evidence in its favour. Sadly, this is salted with superstitious fables. Even more sadly, the site and the surroundings have been changed beyond recognition, and all physical evidence is destroyed—including the hill and the tomb! Modern archaeological maps also mark a point on the Mount of Olives opposite the Eastern Gate as a likely site for the crucifixion, and therefore perforce for the resurrection, since the tomb was in a garden 'at the place where Jesus was crucified' (John 19:41).

I would sometimes begin my talk with a slightly tongue-in-cheek challenge. 'It is easier to prove that Jesus of Nazareth rose from the dead than to prove that George Washington ever lived.' (The example would vary according to the nationality of the audience—Julius Caesar, Oliver Cromwell, Attila the Hun, Frederick the Great, etc.).

Slightly teasing, but fair. Historical knowledge depends on a combination of written eyewitness accounts, records of contemporary debate, observation of the results flowing from the alleged events, and a consideration of what are called 'memorials and customs'.

The Gunpowder Plot of 1605 may serve as an example. We have letters and diaries of the plotters and details of the interrogation and trial. The consequences of the plot and its failure are obvious enough (and still regretted by voters disillusioned with Parliament!). As for memorials and customs, we celebrate Guy Fawkes Night on November 5th, and the church of St Michael-le-Belfry in York has a plaque marking the baptism of the chief character.

Of course none of this produces infallible certainty, but without it historical knowledge would be impossible.

Facing the facts

Apply these criteria to the Easter Story. We have written records of a quality that students of most ancient history can only dream of. We know plenty about the furious debates aroused by the event (inside and outside the Bible). As for the results flowing from the event, they are indisputable. Christianity did emerge and flourish, with the Resurrection as its central message. Her first witnesses were utterly convinced, and soon persuaded thousands of others. In twentieth century paraphrase, we could say that any shorthand typist could have scuppered the whole movement at birth by taking a ten-minute walk during her lunch break and running back with the cry, 'It's a lot of nonsense. I've just checked the tomb and he's dead.'

For memorials and customs, we have the two sacraments of baptism and communion, observed ever since. Both symbolise the death and resurrection of Christ. And we have the remarkable shift of the Jewish 'Sabbath' to the Christian 'Lord's Day' to mark the day he rose. All of the first Christians were Jews; what lesser event could have brought about such a fundamental change in their calendar?

It is a fascinating theme. Those who wish to pursue it are recommended to read carefully one of the books devoted to weighing the evidence.[3] A favourite quotation of mine comes from a high court judge who can be presumed to know something about the rules of evidence: 'The case for the resurrection of Christ is overwhelming. I have secured verdicts in court on far less evidence.'[4]

Five versions, one event
The four Gospel writers and the Apostle Paul provide their accounts, fascinating in impact, differing in detail, convincing in their cumulative effect.[5]

---

3. For example Michael Green, *Man Alive* and John McDowell, *The Resurrection Factor*.

4. Lord Caldecote, Lord Chief Justice of England. Quoted by McDowell, page 11, from Linton H Irwin, *A Lawyer Examines The Bible*, Baker Book House, page 14.

5. *Five resurrection accounts:* Matthew 28; Mark 16:1-8; Luke 24; John 20 & 21; 1 Corinthians 15:1-8.

All insist on stark physical facts. There is little room here for some spiritual or metaphorical interpretation. The cross, the nails, the spear, the blood, the wrapping-cloths, the spices, the tomb, the stone and the guards; here are the details of physical death and burial. But exactly the same kind of detail continues into the events of Easter morning. The stone is rolled away, the guards flee, the tomb is empty, the women with spices find no body, the wrapping-cloths lie discarded, Jesus appears and points to his own scars in hands and side.

Yet all is *not* quite the same. Jesus is rarely recognised at first. At least once he appears through locked doors. At least once he disappears abruptly. Mary mistakes him for a gardener, Cleopas thinks he is a stranger to Jerusalem, the disciples in their boat take some time to recognise him on the shore. There is an odd 'otherness' as well as a familiarity about him.

And what of those apparent contradictions? It is hard (many say impossible) to put the five stories in some cohesive order. Did the women arrive at the tomb in the dark or after sunrise? How many women were there? How many angels met them? Did the women believe the evidence? Did the men believe the women? When did the subsequent 'appearances' happen, and in what order? Critical (and even friendly) readers use phrases like 'glaring contradictions' and 'abandon all idea of harmonizing'. Any attempt to put the clues together is made to sound like a task in which Sherlock Holmes, Father Brown and Hercule Poirot would exhaust their combined efforts.

But odd though it may sound, I have often used the problem as an argument in favour of the basic truthfulness of the varied stories.

Every policeman and magistrate can smell a cooked-up tale. One sure sign of it is total agreement between professedly independent witnesses. Genuine witnesses will often sound contradictory, simply because each has a partial experience and knowledge, and each tells it from a different standpoint. Patient questioning will establish the whole truth. Conversely, a false agreed alibi or conspiracy will sound plausible on the surface, but begins to crumble during an in-depth interrogation. As John Wenham says in his *Easter Enigma:*

> The resurrection stories exhibit in a remarkable way the well-known characteristics of accurate and independent reporting, for superficially they show great disharmony, but on close examination the details gradually fall into place.[6]

A striking fact often overlooked is that *we have no description of the resurrection.* The Gospel writers describe its immediate consequences. The stone moved, the guards frightened, the tomb empty, the grave cloths scattered—this is not a picture of the event but of its aftermath. Writers of fiction would have found the invitation irresistible, and would oblige with details: the sudden stirring of breath, a shaft of light, some heavenly music. But Matthew and his friends are not writing fiction. They record *facts*—and the fact is that visitors found an empty tomb, heard a mysterious message, and

6. Wenham, page 11. This book well repays careful reading. After detailed examination of the stories, to the length of pacing out the distances with a timepiece and examining the topography, the author concludes, 'When every effort has been made to give the details of the narratives their full weight, they add up to a consistent story', page 124.

subsequently met the risen Jesus. No-one saw the rising, and no-one attempts to describe it. Later writers did make pious attempts, of course. Their efforts, always recognized as a kind of second-century religious thriller, are in marked contrast to the Gospel story:

> In the night there rang out a loud voice in heaven - the stone started of itself to roll and gave way to the side - three men came out from the sepulchre, and two of them sustaining the other, and a cross following them. The heads of the two reached to heaven but that of the third overpassed the heavens (The apocryphal Gospel of Peter).[7]

This is exactly what the New Testament does *not* give us. The accounts are sober, restrained and honest. The women visitors, the wider circle of disciples and 'the eleven' themselves were not immediately convinced. But eventually they became so—and staked their lives on it.

I believe in Christ's resurrection *because* the first Christians, nearest the facts, became convinced, *because* the tomb was clearly empty when the church began, *because* alternative explanations of the disciples' conviction and the tomb's vacancy totally fail in their purpose. I believe it *because* the kind of evidence available for any widely accepted historical fact is available for this supreme fact.

But there is a further reason: one given by every Christian. I believe in the resurrection because I have tasted something

---

7. The Gospel of Peter 9, 10 quoted from New Testament Apocrypha volume 1.

of the risen life of Christ. It is the argument of experience.

And at this point we do indeed move from the area of physically ascertainable fact to a different kind of area that defies definition. The empty tomb is not the foundation of our faith: it is a sign and symbol of something vaster than any merely physical fact. No-one can visit the tomb with any certainty today. Even if they could, its physical emptiness *now* would prove nothing. The risen Christ (who undoubtedly left the tomb empty, ate with his disciples and 'showed them his hands and his side') is not seen physically today, but with the eye of faith. With the apostle Paul, every Christian says, 'Christ lives in me. The life I live in the body, I live by faith in the Son of God who loved me, and gave himself for me' (Galatians 2:20).

Although historical enquiry and 'apologetics' is helpful and necessary, the Christian witnessing to his faith today is not really taking the part of a lawyer presenting a case to a jury who must surely come to the correct verdict if they are given enough reliable facts. My little lectures at the Garden Tomb aroused interest, encouraged searching, and in some cases prompted the beginnings of faith. But people every day come into a first-time encounter with the Living Christ through *the presentation of himself in his gospel.*

This, surely, is the real significance of those words addressed to doubting Thomas a week after the resurrection.

Then he said to Thomas, 'Put your fingers here; see my hands. Reach out your hand and put it into my side. Stop doubting and believe.'

Thomas said to him, 'My Lord and my God!'

Then Jesus told him, 'Because you have seen me, you

have believed; blessed are those who have not seen and yet have believed' (John 20:27-29).

We easily misunderstand this story. Jesus (I believe) was not saying, 'It was fairly easy for you to believe. You have seen the evidence. But it is harder for those who don't see the evidence nevertheless to believe. So there is an extra word of praise for them.'

Rather (surely) he was saying, 'Theirs is the normal way to come to faith, and therefore truly blessed.' Neither a physically empty tomb nor an occasional mysterious 'appearance' can be the normal way to find the Risen Christ. Rather, we discover him in our response to his gospel invitation.

Several other 'appearance stories' say the same thing, once we have the clue. Mary misunderstood the evidence, and thought she was talking to a gardener. It was her personal name, spoken with love and power, as it had once commanded the seven demons to leave her, that brought her to a passion of faith and love. He still calls us by name (John 20:1-18).

The sight of the living Jesus by the lake, even the repetition of a familiar command to let down the net, did not convince Peter. It was the reminder of the charcoal fire where he failed, and the call to a fresh commitment of love that won him to love and service. That call still comes to us, in our failure and perplexity (John 21:1-19).

The two on the road to Emmaus (not members of the closest circle) entirely failed to 'get it together' simply through a sight of the resurrected Master. What convinced them was an extended, conversational Bible study and the prayer as he 'broke bread' with them at table (with obvious sacramental implications). 'Were not our hearts burning within us while

he talked with us on the road and opened the Scriptures to us?'
(Luke 24:13-35). Jesus was recognised by them when he broke
the bread.

I have certainly sat by the Emmaus road and found that the
words of Scripture 'warmed' my heart. I have stood on what
is almost certainly the site of the Last Supper, and 'recognised' my Saviour with faith and love. But no-one needs to
travel to Jerusalem for that experience—as every Christian,
who searches the Bible prayerfully and partakes of Communion believingly, knows.

Walking with Jesus today means reading his words, welcoming the impact of his personality, struggling to understand
the import of his challenge, embracing the provision he makes
through his death and resurrection. Sharing his good news
with others involves presenting them with the facts, but also
living before them a life consistent with his principles.

Chapter 11

The Man who Throws Down the Challenge

The town of Caesarea Philippi stands on the southern slope of the great mountain range of Hermon, that 9,000 foot snow-capped peak from which most of Israel's water sources flow. The area today links the borders of Israel, Syria and Lebanon.

It was old, but newly named in Jesus' day. Philip Herod had enlarged and beautified it. Doffing his hat to his political master, the Emperor Tiberius (Caesar), he added his own name in self-congratulation (Philippi). The puppet-king's reign was destined to end in AD 34, very near to the time when Jesus stood in the sloping streets and drew together the cords of his Galilee ministry by asking at its close, 'Who do you say I am?'

Simon Peter's famous reply has sounded like a trumpet down through the centuries. 'You are the Christ, the Son of the Living God' (Matthew 16:13-28).

As with so many other Gospel scenes, the topography casts fascinating light and adds to the impression of a historical event that 'really happened that way'. Standing there, Bible in hand, one feels, 'It happened here, and it could have happened nowhere else in quite this way.'

The other name of the town was Panias, so called because a shrine to Pan, the god of nature, stood there. Our word *panic*, originally meaning superstitious fear, comes from it. The modern Arab name almost preserves the word (as so often happens); today it is called Banyas, as the Arabic tongue has difficulty with the letter P.

Superstitious fear was indeed the hallmark of Caesarea Philippi. Herod the Great with his usual cynical balancing of Jewish belief and pagan political realism had already erected a pagan temple of white marble, dedicated to Caesar Augustus. Cut into the cliff walls were niches and statues to various gods, forming a *pantheon* (notice the word again). Within a hundred yards of the pantheon a gaping cave in the hillside, the size of a railway tunnel, slopes downwards out of sight. Its ancient name, the Paneion Cave, once again recalls that word. Jews in this pagan area of northern Galilee derisively called it the Gate of Hades (or Hell)—partly because pagans considered it the doorway to the Underworld, and partly because the Jews understood the powers behind the pantheon to be demonic.

All of these features are echoed in the famous exchange between Jesus and Peter.

The town had strategic importance too. If not the cross-roads, it was certainly the T-junction of the northern Middle East. Westward ('left') the road ran to the Mediterranean ports of Syro-Phoenicia, crucial to trade, tribute and military deployment, and thence northwards into Roman Asia where Paul would soon be planting churches. Eastwards ('right') was the 'Road to Damascus' and beyond to the Persian empire. Southwards from the Panias junction, the highway ran 'down' the Galilee Pan-handle, skirting Capernaum on the lakeside (tax centre for the province) and then turning westwards along the Valley of Jezreel, past Megiddo (Armageddon) and then southwards again as the great *Via Maris*, the coast road to Egypt.

See now how breathtakingly appropriate was the challenge of Jesus: Who do people say that I am? Who do *you* say that I am?

Here is the implicit launching of a world mission along the world's highways. Here is the implicit challenge to the world's political and religious powers. Here, at the source of the Holy Land's water supply, is the challenge to the identity of Israel's faith and hope. Here is the challenge of the Christ-King's unique authority—and the announcement of his purpose.

'Who do you say I am?'

'You are the Christ, the Son of the Living God.'

'On this rock I will build my church, and the gates of Hades will not overcome it'(Mark 8:27-30, Matthew 16:18).

Jesus began to explain that he must be killed and on the third day raised to life.

The scene makes a fitting climax to our sketch of the Evangelist who is indeed the Evangel; the Messenger who is himself the Message. It reminds us of the claims of this unique Person. It sums up the reasons why Christians recognise him as the very image of the unseen God, in stark contrast to the idol-images of Herod Philip's day and our own.

It also poses the question once more: *Does Christ's church today reflect at least something of the character, the message and the methods of its founder and Lord?*

Modern scholars often pre-empt the whole question by asserting that the church-building promise was never in fact uttered by Jesus, here or anywhere else. They point out that

Mark's original account of the incident never mentions 'church'. They point out that the very word in fact only appears three times on the lips of Jesus in the Gospel records, each time in Matthew's Gospel which bears all the hallmarks of being a church manual. They suggest (even insist) that all three references are examples of the early Christian habit of 'writing back' its own developed reflection and practice into the Jesus-story.

There is no need at all to be so dismissive. The Greek word *ecclesia* (translated into English as *church*, here and throughout the New Testament) is the equivalent of the Hebrew word *quahal,* which is presumably the word that Jesus actually used. This is employed repeatedly in the Old Testament to describe *Israel gathered for instruction and worship.* The word means *gathered congregation.* In its Greek form it was also used to describe a town council gathered to exercise authority. Stephen, the first known Christian martyr, used it in that Jewish sense when he spoke of 'the church in the wilderness' (Acts 7:38 AV) or 'the assembly in the desert'. Later apostolic use spoke of the church as the local congregation of committed disciples, or the worldwide church made up of members from every nation, class and colour (Acts 8:1; Ephesians 5:23).

All of those *concepts* appear constantly in the teaching of Jesus, not only when he is recorded as using the actual word 'church'. His choice of precisely *twelve* closest disciples was full of symbolism: they represented the twelve tribes of God's called-out congregation Israel. His numerous examples of reaching out to the dispossessed, the unclean and the Gentile prefigured that enlargement of Israel to include many others within the people of God. The famous (if infuriating) words about people coming from east and west to the divine banquet with Abraham, Isaac and Jacob, and the grim warning that the Kingdom would be taken from one group and offered to another; these and similar sayings all expressed the same intention to 'build my church'. The solemn words about a 'new covenant', echoing old prophetic promise, but now associated with the bread and wine of the Last Supper say the same.[1]

So we need not ask, 'Did Jesus ever plan to build a church?' What we do need to ask is *'did he plan it to be anything like this?'* (pointing to what we see today). Is this what he wanted? Would he be disappointed at the outcome?

To put it in a slightly different way—'Is today's Christian life and witness, individual and corporate, a reasonable reflection, *first* of the good news Christ offered, *second* of the life it is said to produce, and *thirdly* of the methods used in its propagation?'

What Jesus displays

Looking at the human figure of Jesus we see three things which establish our knowledge of God, shape our lifestyles, and inform our message to the world in which we live.

In Jesus we see what God is like. Through Jesus we are brought into a new way of living. From Jesus we receive a commission to make disciples for him in all the world. Let me put it slightly differently by making several propositions.

---

1. Jesus and his church: Mark 3:14-19; Matthew 8:11; 21:41; Luke 22:19-20.

(1) Seeing Jesus, we see God

Jesus shows us God in action. He is recorded as asking one of his closest circle, 'Don't you know me, Philip, even after I have been among you such a long time? Anyone who has seen me has seen the Father. How can you say, show us the Father?' (John 14:8-9).

In other words, Jesus gives concrete expression to what would otherwise be an abstraction (powerfully true, but somehow lacking visible reality that can be grasped). We are *told* that God is love, God is light, God is holy, and so on. But in the life, words and deeds of Jesus we *see* it. Propositional truth becomes visible action.

Watch him welcoming children, kneeling beside a threatened adulteress, commending a widow, inviting himself to lunch with a crooked local government officer, embracing a leper, restoring sanity to a demoniac—here is love, light and holiness defined in human action.

As Marcus Borg says:

He did not reveal God only in his teaching (as if revelation consists primarily of *information*), but in his very way of being. The epiphany was *Jesus*—his person as well as his message—what he was like therefore discloses what God is like.[2]

This is what New Testament writers later expressed in various (inspired) ways.

The Word was with God in the beginning—The Word

---

2. Borg, page 191. I do not follow every conclusion reached by this author, but he speaks powerfully about the true humanity of Jesus.

became flesh and made his dwelling among us. We have seen his glory.

Being in very nature God—he made himself nothing—being made in human likeness.

The Son is the radiance of God's glory and the exact representation of his being (John 1:1, 14; Philippians 2:6-7; Hebrews 1:3).

Christians call this the Incarnation. That means (literally) God coming here in human flesh. The theology works both ways. Jesus does not simply give us hints as to what God is like because he got closer to God than anyone else. He shows us what God is like because *when we look at him we are looking at God.* Christ's compassion for sufferers is not a replica or reminder of God's compassion—it *is* God's compassion, for he is God.

But equally, Jesus is really human. As John says Jesus *became* flesh. He crossed a boundary into an authentic human experience which he did not previously have. Jesus was not God in disguise; he was God in the flesh. He did not simply visit this planet; he became one of us.

> In that humanity he felt pleasure and pain, as we feel pleasure and pain. In that human nature he laughed and cried, hoped and feared, knew delight and disappointment. The mystery and message of the incarnation is that in Jesus, God acquired manhood and the deity became a member of the human race.[3]

So Peter Lewis puts it. He is right.

---

3. Peter Lewis, page 124.

(2) Trusting Jesus, we find God

But the glory of the gospel shines further and wider. Jesus did not come to make us all theologians. He came to introduce us to God. Knowing what God is like will only plunge us into despair unless we can find our way back to him through the barriers of sin, failure, fear and guilt. Paul tells us that 'God was in Christ, reconciling the world to himself' (2 Corinthians 5:19 AV). That was achieved both by his life and his death.

Dozens of episodes in his life illustrate and encapsulate God's reconciling purpose. His healing miracles spoke not only of physical-mental wholeness, but of restoration to the community of God's people. His meals with the marginalised announced a Kingdom open to all. His suffering confronted and shamed those power systems that deny true humanity by claiming a false deity. The shedding of his lifeblood paid the ransom-price that sets us free to be God's children.

In all of this it is equally important to see him as truly human and truly divine. If Jesus is not God, then God himself has not come to us; he has simply sent someone else. But if he is not God *in our flesh* then God may 'know' with divine omniscience what pain, fear, loneliness and disappointment are 'like', but he does not know it as experience and feeling. But equally, if God's coming in Jesus was not really a coming into true humanity, then his pain, fear, loneliness and disappointment (not to mention his temptations) were only apparent, not real. The inspired writer would not then be able to say:

> He too shared in their humanity so that by his death he might destroy him who holds the power of death .... He had to be made like his brothers in every way .... that he might make atonement for the sins of the people ....

Because he himself suffered when he was tempted, he is
able to help those who are being tempted (Hebrews 2:14-
18).

> It is only because we can sing of—
> our God contracted to a span,
> incomprehensibly made *man,*
> —that we can add—
> Amazing love, how can it be,
> that thou, my *God,* shouldst die for me!

(3) Following Jesus, we please God

To non-Christians, the *example* of Jesus comprises the most
obvious thing about him. They often lift words and episodes
from the story at random, to illustrate a particular virtue
which they admire. 'Turn the other cheek', 'Put love first',
'Despise hypocrisy', 'Always be tolerant', 'Never condemn',
'Side with the poor', and so on. Some of this he never actually
said; other sayings are quoted with no sense of context or
purpose. They add up to no coherent picture.

For different reasons, Evangelical Christians also struggle
with the idea of example. They rightly insist that Christ offers
a way of salvation, not a code of conduct. Their whole
understanding of *grace* seems threatened by any suggestion
that we please God by trying to imitate Christ. He did not die
on a cross to show us *how to live,* but to *give us life.*

Yet we are left with a question. In that case what was Jesus'
life and example *for*? What did he *mean* by calling people to
follow him? After all, the great evangelistic commission is a
call to discipling, baptism and *obedience* (Matthew 28:19-20).

Some suggest that the life of Jesus was designed to

convince us of our moral failure and thus make us aware of our
need for forgiveness and salvation. The glaring contrast
between him and us drives us to repentance. Clearly there is
some truth in this; I have seen it happen. But it does offer a
rather stilted and artificial way of looking at Jesus' life. It
almost gives the impression of a performance whose true
motive is not goodness for the sake of goodness. In any case,
is it not the purpose of *the Law of God* to make us aware of our
sin? (Romans 7:7-13).

Some 'Dispensationalists' offer another approach[4]. They
suggest that Jesus' life and ministry is not our concern in this
Gospel Age. Jesus offered the Kingdom (in himself, the King)
to those for whom it was promised. They rejected it by failing
to recognize him. God overruled; and through the crucifixion
wrought out a means of salvation offered to all. One day, when
the gospel offer is closed, Christ will return and the Jews will
be offered the Kingdom once more. *Then* such teaching as the
Sermon on the Mount will be put into practice. It is the model
for the Millennium. The original Scofield Bible presented the
Sermon on the Mount as a mixture of Law and Grace not fully

---

4. *Dispensationalism*. A system of theology popularised by early
Brethren writers and by the Scofield Reference Bible. It sees all human
history as divided into epochs or 'dispensations' in each of which God
speaks, but from each of which comes human apostasy and failure. So,
for example, Eden ended with the Fall, Noah's time ended with the
Flood, and even the Millennium will end in rebellion. The Church Age
will end in religious apostasy ushering in the Return of Christ.
Dispensationalists tend to interpret scriptures in a uniformly literalis-
tic manner, regardless of their literary form as poetry, apocalyptic,
parable or whatever. In the USA the system is regarded by most
Fundamentalists as synonymous with biblical Christianity. The writings of Hal Lindsay are a popular version of Dispensationalism.

appropriate to the Dispensation of Grace.

Acute problems are raised by this approach and it finds little acceptance today. The gospel of grace preached by the apostles after Pentecost cannot be a different message from the good news of the Kingdom proclaimed by Jesus, the twelve and the seventy-two before the crucifixion. Details may differ because of circumstance and time, but there is only one gospel, and attempts to find two (or even three or four) do no service to Christ's cause. In fact most Dispensationalists have preached and lived better than that!

The Upside-down Kingdom

An Evangelical approach that takes the life and ministry of Jesus more seriously (yet still puts his death and resurrection at the centre) might go something like this.

Jesus offered the Kingdom by offering himself as the fulfilment of God's Kingdom-promises. Its life-principles were personified in himself, for he perfectly lived out the will of God. That life turns upside down the values and priorities of his society and ours.

Under God's rule, people remain unseduced by personal possessions, but act against the poverty of others. They forswear the dark pleasures of revenge and turn the other cheek to those who offend them. They abandon the clamour for their own rights and win their way by meekness. They abandon the search for personal gratification, and hunger and thirst after goodness. They turn from vain ideas of putting God in their debt and cast themselves on his love and grace. They subdue the constant urge to put people into categories according to class, colour, sex, race, religion or achievement, and pioneer new kinds of barrier-breaking community. They refuse the seductive lure of power manipulation and win others by humble service.

Such a lifestyle can never be attained by human willpower or effort. It is entered through a radical change called repentance, and the gift of a new heart through rebirth. With new attitudes and values, we come under the reign of God, who offers to be our Father. Jesus not only personified that Kingdom in his own life, but he broke the barriers to God that keep us under Satan's sway, by dying and rising again. The gift of his Spirit brings us into God's power and grace.

It is of such a Kingdom that the apostles spoke. As the message broke through into the non-Jewish world, they employed less Kingdom language, and spoke more of 'gospel', 'salvation', and 'church'. But this in no way made their message any different from that of Jesus.[5] There only is and only ever will be 'one gospel'. The Christian who lives this out with some consistency is proclaiming the good news. The community that displays these attributes with some consistency is a gospel church, whatever label it wears.

(4) Imitating Jesus, we serve God

This is yet more challenging. It returns us to the question, 'Would Jesus recognize and own today's church?' Do our compassionate influence and our missionary endeavours reflect the motives and methods of our Master?

Christ brought truth with persuasion (see chapters 1 & 2). Today the very concept of truth is denied. All is relative. You may believe what is authentic to you, but you may not question anyone else's self-authentic system. Christian teachers can

---

5. The Kingdom in later apostolic teaching, Acts 28:28-31; Colossians 1:13.

have no truck with such subjectivism. If this makes them sound intolerant (the one unforgivable sin in today's society), then so be it. Jesus' words 'I am the truth—no-one comes to God except by me' sound fairly intolerant!

On the other hand, Jesus laboured to *communicate* that unchanging truth, with a skill born of empathy. He mustered illustration, humour, analogy, parable, poetry, precept, logic and emotion, because (to coin an ungrammatical but useful phrase) 'he understood where people were at'. We must do the same. The church needs spokesmen and apologists who understand and address people's perceived needs and situations, rather than talking into the vacuum of where they think we ought to be. Jesus came to *seek* and to save.

I fear for churches whose leaders (however defined, appointed and deployed) do not major on this alliance of truth and communication. Mere orthodox phrases, however faithfully delivered, do not automatically carry authority and anointing; *that* comes from the Holy Spirit. On the other hand, slick communication skills and applied church-growth principles may gain a hearing (even a temporary following), but they will not build God's Kingdom unless they convey divine *truth*. I tremble when I hear of ministerial selection boards who appear to be seeking skills appropriate to a social worker who moonlights as a TV quiz-show presenter! Some of our most 'successful' evangelical churches are already showing signs of the famine of God's Word that follows.

Jesus broke barriers and mended people (see chapters 3 & 4). He saw no-one as hopelessly and irredeemably 'outside'. Nor must we. In Christ's community there is no room for class distinction, colour bar, racial prejudice, age gap or culture clash. That is the theory! In actual fact many churches are split on issues as superficial as physical stance at prayer, musical instruments in worship, or clothes worn in church. What hope is there of commending a barrier-breaking gospel to a torn and polarised society?

On the other hand, Evangelicals need not be too ashamed of their attitude to *people*. They may arouse fury in the Permissive Establishment for insisting that *family* has a divine blueprint or that homosexuality and adultery are sins. But evangelical agencies, as a matter of simple fact, deploy more ministry to the homeless and give more care to Aids victims than all the other voluntary agencies put together. Christ's call is to mend people, as well as to tell them truth.

Jesus exposed the powers (see chapters 8 & 9). The structures that held power in his day, whether political, religious or economic, failed to intimidate, confuse or seduce him. His life, words and actions challenged their worldly priorities and exposed their satanic deceptions.

We Christians in the West have watched and prayed as churches in Russia, Africa, Asia and South America have fought their battles against their equivalents of Pilate, Herod and Caiaphas. In recent amazing years one power after another has self-destructed—Marxism, Nationalism, Apartheid and so on. In the process, Christians and churches there have responded with varying degrees of compromise, resistance, protest or passive suffering. From our safe position, who are we to presume to judge or assess?

But we must judge ourselves, in our own situation. How deeply has our western church been corrupted by market amorality? by blatant secularism in education, medicine and entertainment? by media manipulation or sexual compromise?

How enthusiastically have we embraced and christened the cult of personal gratification? How widely have our church decision-making bodies (national or local) reflected techniques and attitudes that stand in stark contrast to the Servant King who washed his disciples' feet? How far have our methods of ministerial selection and assessment veered in the direction of cynical, secular man-management and perform-ance-orientated models that are alien to the spirit of Christ and his gospel?

In his final chapter (*Jesus As Challenge*) Marcus Borg has a searching paragraph.

Taking the vision of Jesus seriously calls the church to be an alternative culture in our time. Though there may have been periods in the history of the West when its 'official' values roughly coincided with the central values of the Christian tradition, that time is no more. In the modern period, a yawning gap has opened.

The dominant features of contemporary American life—affluence, achievement, appearance, power, com-petition, consumption, individualism—are vastly dif-ferent from anything recognizably Christian. [6]

This is painfully true, within the church almost as clearly as without. For great numbers of American Christians, those false values would feature largely in a list of Christian virtues. That is markedly so amongst Evangelicals, Fundamentalists and Charismatics. The list could be incorporated into the agenda of the Christian Right (admittedly with some addi-

6. Borg, pages 194-5 (my italics).

tional biblical thinking about family and human life). It could stand on its own as a succinct summary of the aims of many televangelists (simply add the name Jesus, and stir briskly). It sounds like a page from the publicity of the Prosperity Gospel movement. I have met hundreds of Christians, sincere, devout and committed to Jesus and his gospel, who would put their name to those 'dominant features'.

And not only in America. The other side of the Atlantic is not fundamentally different—only 'more so'. The same yawning gap, in Borg's words, has opened in British Christianity.

So we are left with the challenge. Without doubt, Jesus of Nazareth is all that he claims to be. He is the Christ of God, the Saviour of mankind, the Lord of the Church. But is our portrayal of him, in word and deed, anything like Good News?

Appendix

The Chronology of Jesus and the Gospels

Nothing vital to saving faith depends on knowing exactly when Jesus was born and when the Gospels were written. The modern demand for instant information and precise chronology creates a feeling of certainty that is quite illusory. One personal eyewitness of (say) a military battle has no chance at all of really 'seeing what goes on', let alone of understanding it. Would a Paris spectator of the storming of the Bastille have been able to give a coherent and explicable account of the French Revolution? Of course not. Would we understand the gospel of Christ crucified more fully if we had a glimpse of Pontius Pilate's diary for Good Friday, written up and dated that night? Would a Passover edition of Jerusalem's first-century equivalent of *The Sun* give us a surer faith in the Risen Saviour? Hardly.

Nevertheless, Christians believe that, in Jesus, God stepped into the stream of human history to redeem mankind. Clearly some rough idea of the when-and-where is useful. 'Some idea' is all we have, for a number of reasons.

Needless to say, no-one knew that they lived so-many-years 'BC' (Before Christ) when the event had not yet happened! The entire system of BC and AD depends on calculations made several centuries after the events. Nor was there a previous universally-accepted system of reckoning to which it could be simply adjusted. People recorded events in relationship to other events (e.g. 'the year after the great

163

earthquake'). Or they linked the passage of time to the reigns of powerful rulers (e.g. 'the fourth year of Caesar Augustus'). Several links of this kind are found in the Old Testament, and at least one in the New offers us a date of sorts for the start of Jesus' public ministry.

Sometimes several different events are interlinked, rather in the style of a modern map-maker giving several different bearings, to locate where they coincide. Luke does this, providing us with the names of Judaea's governor, Galilee's King and Jerusalem's high-priesthood, all corresponding to 'the fifteenth year of the reign of Tiberius Caesar' (Luke 3:1-2). That is still not precise. Does the fifteenth year mean 'from the date of his accession' or 'fifteen calendar years after his enthronement' (a choice of fourteen to sixteen years)?

The date of Jesus' birth

Matthew puts this during the reign of Herod the Great (Matthew 2:1-18). Herod died in March or April of 4 BC. Matthew implies that Herod did not live long after his massacre of children in Bethlehem. His final years, in contemporary accounts, certainly manifested the kind of paranoiac violence that the Gospel described. Herod himself set two years earlier as the possible birth of the child ('according to the time he had learned from the Magi' of the star's first appearance). All of this points us to something like 6-8 BC for the birth.

Two astronomical events offer possible explanations of the 'Christmas star' (which is nowhere said to be supernatural in origin). 7 BC saw a twice-repeated conjunction of the planets Jupiter and Saturn, the first time within the constellation Pisces, which was popularly associated with Palestine and Israel. Around 4-5 BC a nova (new star) was sighted by Chinese astronomers. Although this was previously thought not to have been visible in the Middle East, more recent calculations have revised that opinion. None of this is decisive, but it could offer pointers.

Luke adds some facts, but they are not easily interpreted (Luke 2:1-4). There is no record elsewhere of Caesar Augustus organising a universal census. On the other hand, he is known to have been fascinated by tax reform and he reorganized much Roman administration. Egypt was the next Roman Province to Syria, the 'holy land' of Roman times. They had a census every fourteen years, and records survive from the one in AD 20. That would put previous attempts in AD 6 and 8 BC. Did Syria 'stagger' Egypt's programme?

Quirinius, the Syrian governor in Luke's account has caused a few scholarly headaches. He indeed governed Syria —but not as early as 'BC'. Josephus described a census of his in AD 6 (*Antiquities* 18:26) which aroused violent opposition, referred to in Acts 5:37. This date does not fit. But recent research has established that Quirinius had an earlier posting in Syria, as a local military commander. This was from 10-7 BC. Could he have set a census in motion that continued after he left—and which would later be recalled, fairly enough, as the census of *Governor* Quirinius—which by that time he was?

The second-century Christian leader Tertullian puts the 'Christmas census' in 9-6 BC under the Governor Sentius Saturninus. As he lived a good deal nearer the time than we do, perhaps he knew something that we don't!

A date for the birth of Christ is likely between 8 and 4 BC with the best evidence in favour of 7-6 BC.

The ministry of Jesus

Luke's clues, already referred to, furnish a rough guide, since we have independent dates for most of the people he lists. For example, Herod Philip had died by AD 34, and Pontius Pilate's governorship did not begin until AD 26. John's Gospel requires three years' duration for Christ's public ministry. All of this puts the probable date for his arrival in Galilee as AD 29-30, and the crucifixion as AD 32 or 33. Interestingly, several scholars, using different methods of calculation, have come to very much the same conclusion.

How old was Jesus when he died?

Luke describes his public emergence when 'about thirty years old' (Luke 3:23). John makes a surprising comment: only three years later he is described by critics as 'not yet fifty' (John 8:57). However, this was probably an idiomatic phrase: 'He claims to sum up the hopes of the centuries since Abraham, yet he hasn't lived half a century himself' (see the context of the remark).

Putting all of this together, the parameters can now be outlined.

Earliest possible date for Christ's birth - BC 8
Latest possible date for the crucifixion - AD 33
In that case he would be forty-one years old.

Latest possible date for the birth - BC 5
Earliest possible date for the crucifixion - AD 29
This would suggest an age of thirty-four.

Christ's public ministry - an outline

The Gospel writers were more concerned to present impressions than to organise a chronology. Mark gives a broad outline of the Galilee ministry. Luke fills out many details of a long tour of both sides of the Jordan valley. John refers to several periods in Judaea and Jerusalem. All mention visits to Samaria. Matthew and Luke speak of wide sweeps of preaching and ministry north and east into completely pagan territories.

John's frequent references to Jewish feasts provides an outline of seasons, and this is strikingly confirmed by incidental references to weather and vegetation in the other Gospels (especially Mark).

The following is offered as a rough suggested outline.

YEAR 1
January
Baptism of Jesus in Jordan. His first meeting with Peter and several future apostles (Mark 1:9-20).

Early Spring
Having set up home in Capernaum (Galilee) he visits Jerusalem, demonstrates against misuse of the Temple, and gathers disciples (John 1:28-3:21).

Summer and Autumn
After a wider Judaean ministry Jesus returns to Galilee via Samaria. John the Baptist is imprisoned (John 3:22-23; Matthew 14:3-12).

Winter
In Galilee, Jesus gathers 'the Twelve' and draws huge crowds around Capernaum with his teaching and healing (Mark 1:14-45). The Sermon on the Mount (Matthew 5-7).

YEAR 2

Late Winter and early Spring

First mission to Gentile 'Ten Cities' east of Galilee (Mark 5). Rejection of Jesus by his hometown of Nazareth (Luke 4:14-30).

April

Feeding of the 5,000 in Jewish western Galilee (Mark 6:30-44). 'I am the bread of life' (John 6). Probable visit to Jerusalem for Passover.

Summer

Jesus sends the Twelve (perhaps earlier) and then the Seventy-two on widespread missions (Luke 9:1-9; 10:1-24). He himself travels north to pagan Phoenicia and then south and east to Decapolis again, where this time he is welcomed (Mark 7:31-37).

Late Summer

Returning to Jewish Galilee, he rebukes the cities for their failure to repent (Matthew 11:20-30).

September

Jesus visits Jerusalem for the Feast of Tabernacles. He arouses controversy with his teaching and foils an attempt to arrest him (John 7:1-53).

October

Returning to Galilee, he engages in a brief teaching-tour. He then takes the Twelve north to pagan Caesarea Philippi and invites them to confess him as Messiah (Matthew 16). 'I will build my church.' The Transfiguration, probably on mount Hermon (Matthew 17:1-13).

November
Another brief return to Galilee, with a new emphasis on death and resurrection (Matthew 17:14-23).

December
Jesus and his disciples visit Jerusalem for the Feast of Hanukkah, engage in public controversy, and then retire beyond Jordan (John 10:22-42). Perhaps the raising of Lazarus at this time (John 11:1-54).

YEAR 3
Winter and early Spring
Jesus with increasing numbers of disciples travels throughout the Jordan valley (perhaps northwards on the eastern side, and southwards again through Samaria) (Luke 9:51-62). This is the long 'journey to Jerusalem' described by Luke. Many famous parables (Luke 14 and 15).

April
Jesus completes his last journey to Jerusalem, via Jordan and Jericho (healing of blind Bartimaeus and conversion of Zacchaeus the tax-collector) (Luke 18:31-43; 19:1-26). He enters the city on 'Palm Sunday', cleanses the Temple for a second time, and creates a sensation for five days of public teaching and confrontation (Luke 19:28-48). He institutes 'the Lord's Supper' at Passover-eve, is arrested overnight and is crucified on Passover Day (Luke 22-23, John 19).

'The third day he rose again from the dead' ... 'he ascended into heaven' (Luke 24).

May-June
Six weeks later, at the Feast of Pentecost, the Holy Spirit descends and brings the Church to birth (Acts 1, 2).

Book List and References

This is not intended to be a recommended Reading List, less still a Bibliography. It is simply a record of authors quoted or referred to in my 'snapshots' of Jesus' life, work and message. In my footnotes they are referred to simply by the authors' surnames: here the full details of title and publication can be found. It should hardly be necessary to say that my reference to a particular author does not necessarily imply my agreement with his theology or stance.

Hendrick Berkhof, *Christ and the Powers*, translated by John H Yoder, Herald Press, Ontario 1962

Marcus Borg, *Jesus - A New Vision*, SPCK 1993

Craig Blomberg, *The Historical Reliability of the Gospels*, IVP, USA 1987

Donald Bridge, *Living In The Promised Land*, Kingsway 1989

Donald Bridge, *Power Evangelism and The Word of God*, Kingsway 1987

R W Dale, *The Living Christ and the Four Gospels*, Hodder & Stoughton 1891

James D G Dunn, *Jesus' Call to Discipleship*, Cambridge University Press 1992

W R Farmer, *Maccabees, Zealots and Josephus*, Columbia University Press, New York 1956

Dean Farrar, *The Life of Christ*, Cassell & Co. Ltd. 1906

Arnold G Fruchtenbaum, *The Messiah*, Tishrei Magazine, Volume 1, No. 4, Summer 1993

David Gooding, *According To Luke*, IVP 1987

Michael Green, *Man Alive*, IVP, First published 1967. Rewritten as *The Day Death Died* 1982

David Jackman, *Taking Jesus Seriously* (The teaching of Jesus in Matthew), Christian Focus Publications 1994

Joachim Jeremias, *New Testament Theology, Volume 1, The Proclamation of Jesus*, SCM 1971

Jakob Jonsson, *Humour and Irony in the New Testament* (illuminated by parallels in Talmud & Midrash), published by E J Brill, Leider, Netherlands 1985

Flavius Josephus, *The War of the Jews*, modern translation by G A Williamson, Penguin Classics 1959

Peter Lewis, *The Glory of Christ*, Hodder & Stoughton 1992

Josh McDowell, *The Resurrection Factor*, Here's Life Publishers Inc., California 1981

Frank Morison, *Who Moved The Stone?*, Faber & Faber 1930

David Prior, *Jesus and Power*, Hodder & Stoughton 1987 (In the Jesus Library, ed. Michael Green)

David Pytches, *Come, Holy Spirit*, Hodder & Stoughton 1984

Walter Riggans, *Jesus Ben Joseph (An introduction to Jesus the Jew)*, Olive Press (Marc) 1993

Dorothy Sayers, *The Man Born To Be King*, London, Victor Gollanz Ltd. First published May, 1943

Stephen Smalley, *John - Evangelist & Interpreter*, Paternoster, 1978

James S Stewart, *The Life and Teaching of Jesus Christ*, First published, 1933, Church of Scotland Committee on the Religious Instruction of Youth

Joseph Stallings, *Re-discovering Passover (A complete guide for Christians)*, Resource Publications, California 1988

John Stott, IVP, *The Cross of Christ*, first published 1986

Tishrei Magazine. Editor, Clifford Denton, Swansea

Stephen Travis, *I Believe in the Second Coming of Jesus,* Hodder & Stoughton 1982 (In the 'The Jesus Library', ed. Michael Green)

Geza Vermes, *Jesus The Jew and Jesus and the World of Judaism*, SCM Press, 1973 and 1983

John Wenham, *The Easter Enigma*, a Latimer Monograph, 1984. Revised and indexed 1992

Amos N Wilder, *Early Christian Rhetoric - The language of the gospel*, SCM Press 1964

John Wimber, *Power Evangelism and Power Healing*, Hodder & Stoughton 1984 and 1986

Tom Wright, *The Crown and the Fire Meditations on the Cross and the Life of the Spirit*, SPCK 1992

New Testament Apocrypha (2 volumes) Philadelphia: Westminster, 1963, English Translation by R M L Wilson, Lutterworth Press 1963

SPIRITUAL GIFTS AND THE CHURCH

Donald Bridge and David Phypers

First published in the 1970s, when the Charismatic Movement became prominent in British church life, this classic study of gifts, the individual and the church has been revised and expanded in light of developments since then. The authors, Donald Bridge and David Phypers, give a balanced view of a difficult and controversial issue.

The baptism of the Spirit, with its associated gifts, is a subject which has perplexed and fascinated Christians. It is unfortunately one which also divides Christians who disagree over the extent to which gifts should appear in the Church.

Donald Bridge is an evangelist and church consultant with *The Evangelisation Society*, and David Phypers is a Church of England pastor.

192 PAGES   B FORMAT

ISBN 1 85792 141 0

Donald Bridge lives in the city of Durham, England. He is married to Rita: they have two sons and six grandchildren. He is a Baptist minister, now seconded to mission work and leadership consultancy with *The Evangelization Society*. He has pastored three churches and 'planted' several others. Since 1972 he has also written or co-authored fifteen books of popular theology, and made numerous contributions to Scripture Union Bible notes. An expanded and revised edition of one of his titles, *Spiritual Gifts and the Church*, co-authored with David Phypers, is also published by Christian Focus Publications. His spare time interests include walking, sailing, archaeology, reading and stamp collecting. His church membership is currently with Bethany Church in Houghton-le-Spring, near Durham.